MUHAMMADAN FESTIVALS

MUHAMMADAN

FESTIVALS

by

G. E. von Grunebaum

Introduction by C. E. Bosworth

CURZON PRESS : LONDON

Curzon Press Ltd : London and Dublin

First published 1951
Reprinted 1958
New impression 1976
Reprinted 1981

Introduction
© 1976 Curzon Press Ltd

UK 0 7007 0087 0

Printed in Great Britain by offset lithography by
Billing & Sons Ltd, Guildford, London and Worcester

TO MY PARENTS

Introduction

THE AUTHOR OF THIS BOOK, THE LATE
Gustav Edmund von Grunebaum (1909-72) was a tower-
ing figure amongst modern orientalists. His concern
latterly was with the intellectual and cultural history
of Islam, and, more specifically, with the problems of
national awareness and self-identity of contemporary
Muslims in contact with or in reaction against the West.
To all the topics which came under his scrutiny he
brought an urbane, tolerant and sympathetic mind, as
befitted a man who, born and brought up in the Central
European milieu of Habsburg Austria and its successors,
in 1938 uprooted himself for the very different environ-
ment of the United States of America.

When writing upon complicated and delicate currents
of thought such as the interaction between classical and
modern Western culture and Middle Eastern culture,
von Grunebaum sometimes used a somewhat tortuous
English style which seemed at times to combine the
idioms of professorial German and American socio-
logical jargon at its most repellent. But that this style
was consciously adopted as his preferred medium when
discussing complex questions of *Ideengeschichte*, and
was not his habitual style, is amply shown by this present
book, *Muhammadan festivals*, written when von Grunebaum was at the Oriental Institute of the University of
Chicago and before he moved to his final haven of the
Near Eastern Center in the University of California at
Los Angeles. In this book, nothing could be more con-
cise, straightforward and lucid in expression; and a
mastery is displayed in a small compass of a very varied

iii

array of source material, including that of mediaeval Arabic sources, of modern Arab authors on the Meccan Pilgrimage, and of European travellers through the Middle East and observers of the customs and ways of life there.

As von Grunebaum noted at the outset in the Preface to this book, the multifarious forms which the Islamic religious festivals and acts of commemoration have taken, have in the past militated against any western scholar attempting a major work of synthesis on them. On geographical grounds alone, one would expect an immense variation in the embodiments of religious enthusiasm in Morocco and in Central Asia and in Indonesia. Likewise, on the cultural plane, the syncretistic tendencies displayed by Islam in its encounters with the earlier, indigenous faiths of the Balkans or of Black Africa or of the Indo-Pakistan subcontinent, have inevitably influenced the shape and the driving ethos behind these celebrations. The ramifications of a study of this whole subject, one which took into account geographical, ethnic and cultural factors, would probably lead an intending author into a study on the scale of Frazer's *The golden bough*.

Von Grunebaum accordingly preferred to concentrate on the basic features of Islamic religious practice, those of the so-called "Pillars of Islam" like the *salāt* or worship, the *hajj* or Pilgrimage to Mecca and the *saum* or fasting during the month of Ramadān. To this he added a brief but revealing survey of the very characteristic manifestation of popular religious feeling in Islam seen the cult of the Prophet Muhammad, his personality of physical attributes, together with the major events of his life such as the *mīlād* or *maulid an-nabī*, his birthday. He noted, too, the cult of innumerable local saints all over the Islamic world, at whose tombs and shrines the faithful have sought both assistance in the problems of daily life and also intercession for the departed at that time when they will be resurrected for final judgment on the *yaum al-hashr* "Day of gathering-together". Here, more than in any other sphere, the student of comparative religious practices can detect a continuity in belief and behaviour with the preceding and underlying faiths in such regions as the former Christian ones of Palestine, Anatolia and the Balkans. Finally, von Grunebaum appended a chapter on the particular form of emotionalism and religiosity exhibited by the Shī'a sect, with its emphasis on martyrdom and on mourning for members of the house of 'Alī, and its characteristic form of expression in the *ta'ziyas* or passion-plays, one of the few types of dramatic expression in Islam at all comparable with the Western literary form of the drama.

The author provided succinct biographical references for each of his five chapters. In the quarter-century which has elapsed since 1951, there has naturally appeared further literature on the Islamic cult and festivals, an exposition of which would require an undue amount of space. In general, the reader may be referred to the section on Islamic Religion by John B. Taylor in *Middle East and Islam, a bibliographical introduction*, ed. Derek Hopwood and Diana Grimwood-Jones, Inter Documentation Co. AG, Zug 1972, pp. 102-17, and to the relevant articles in the new edition of the *Encyclopaedia of Islām*, Leiden-London 1960- , now up to the letter *K*. The writer of this Introduction may nevertheless be forgiven for adding, in this age of emphasis on feminism and on women's assuming their rightful place in the world, two interesting references. One is the book of Winifred Steger, *Life with Ali*, Angus and Robertson, Sydney 1969, the story of how the Chinese half-caste wife of an Indian Muslim made the Pilgrimage from Australia to Mecca in 1927, and the other is the article of Michael E. Jansen, "An American girl on the Hajj", in *Aramco World magazine*, XXV/6 (Nov.-Dec. 1974), pp. 31-9, the story of an American Muslim convert's Pilgrimage.

Manchester 1976   C. E. BOSWORTH

Preface

IT IS PERHAPS NOT SURPRISING THAT
Western scholars have not made as systematic a study of
the religious festivals of the Islamic world as of those of
other religions. Colorful as these festivals are and rich in
interpretative material, they present endless ramifications
in terms of the history and psychology of religion over
many centuries and in many diverse parts of the world.
These ramifications are not easily fitted into one simple
coordinated system, nor has Western scholarship so far
attempted to do so.

This book, therefore, does not pretend to be a complete
study of the festivals of Islam. The presentation here has
been concerned with the essential and typical elements
of Islamic ritual, rather than the particularities of any one
sect, any one period, or any one nationality. In other
words, it hopes to contribute to a portrayal of the typical Muslim as a practicing believer by showing him at
prayer, on Pilgrimage, or in the act of honoring his saints.

The diverse levels of his religious experience are en-
visaged in greater detail than are the variations of local
custom, produced by folk tradition, outside the heartlands
of Islam. More than thirteen centuries of Muslim life have
been roamed through freely in an endeavor to impress
upon the reader the coexistence, in the Islamic experience,
of elements of different cultural ancestry, unequal in age
and spiritual worth. The integration of these different elements results in that peculiar style of life and thought which

is the ultimate tangible reality of Islamic civilization and which seems to take body rather strikingly in the complexities of its festivals.

The illustrations are meant to counteract the inevitable abstractness of mere description. If they serve their purpose, this will be due in large measure to Dr. Richard Ettinghausen, Freer Gallery of Art, Washington, D. C., who generously assisted in the selection of the miniatures.

G.E.V.G.
Chicago, Illinois

Contents

Introduction *iii*

Preface *vii*

About the spelling of Arabic words *xiii*

I · The Foundations of Islam *3*
Prayer and the Friday Service

II · Pilgrimage *15*

III · Ramadân *51*

IV · The Prophet and the Saints *67*

V · The Tenth of Muharram *85*

Bibliographical Notes and References *95*

Index *103*

Illustrations

facing page

1. The *Masjid al-Haram*, Mecca 16

2. Muhammad with 'Alî and other companions at the Ka'ba 16

3. Plan of the *Haram* of Mecca and the *Mas'à* 16

4. The *Haram* with the Ka'ba from the northeast 17

5. The *Bâb as-Safâ*, facing toward the Hill of Safâ 32

6. The road between Mecca, Minà and 'Arafa 33

7. The Mount of Mercy in 'Arafa 48

8. Minà 48

9. The stoning of the Second Devil in Minà 49

10. The *Masjid al-Khaif* in Minà 49

11. Looking for the new moon at the end of Ramadân 64

12. The Indian Emperor Jahângîr (1605-27), attending mosque at the *'id al-fitr* 65

13. Mosque scene 80

14. The Mystic Dance of a Sûfî fraternity 81

About the spelling of Arabic words

ARABIC WORDS ARE ACCURATELY TRANS-
literated. The spelling of English words derived from
Arabic names will approximate the original form as closely
as possible. Therefore, *Muhammadan* is chosen rather than
the more common Mohammedan. On the other hand, the
conventional spelling *Mecca* is retained since it renders
adequately the sound of Arabic *Makka*.

In the transliteration, ' stands for the glottal stop that is
audible, for instance, in the phrase *an hour* before the
vowel of the second word. *dh* is the English *th* in *that*, *kh*
the Scottish *ch* in *loch*, *gh* a guttural not represented in
English but somewhat like the French *r grasséyé; q* indicates a strongly articulated guttural *k*. For technical reasons "emphatic" articulation of *d, s, t,* and *z* has not been
marked, nor has the sharp guttural in *Muhammad* or *hajj*
(corresponding to the Hebrew ח) been distinguished
from *h*. ' (the Hebrew ע) is another strong guttural
related to ח —both are practically unpronounceable to
Western tongues.

Muhammadan Festivals

★

i . *The Foundations of Islam*

PRAYER AND THE FRIDAY SERVICE

ISLAM WAS BORN IN ONE OF THE BACKWARD
areas of the ancient world. The radical monotheism of
its doctrine and the puritanism of its mood, combined
with the esthetic limitations of the Muslim's cultural heritage, left the believer satisfied with an arid, if physically
exacting liturgy. Islam either lacked or consciously rejected those elements that elsewhere made for the elaborate
ceremonial sequences of the ecclesiastical year.

An organized Muslim community came into being
within a decade after the prophet Muhammad had begun
to preach and, consequently, Arabic history, other than
that of the Israelites, could not be drawn upon for events
or stages of development deserving religious commemoration. Also Muhammad was a mere man, as his contemporaries well knew and as he himself never ceased to
emphasize. His life was devoid of symbolical ambiguities
and of incidents in which—as in the Last Supper, through
the person of Jesus—the two levels of religious existence
appear to merge and which call for re-enactment as an
illustration or as the culmination of the believer's experience. Nor does Islam recognize sacraments, and this factor
excludes a third motivation for the growth of liturgy.

And, finally, Islam was meant to be a layman's faith.
The absence of a priestly class was bound to restrict the
liturgy in both extent and intricacy. It also limited the
development of festivals and, in general, helped the out-
ward manifestations of Islam to preserve through the ages

3

a curious note of simplicity, even of archaic naïveté, which has long since been eliminated from its theology.

As a result, the festal calendar of Islam originally contained only two festivals: the Pilgrimage or, more precisely, the feast celebrating its successful conclusion; and Fasting in Ramadân, or rather, the feast marking the end of the period of abstention. While the Pilgrimage constitutes a development of the pagan Arab tradition, the Fast adapts a Judaeo-Christian custom. Such festivals as were added later reflect changes in the religious emphasis of the community which, in part, may be accounted for by infiltration of foreign ideas and the reintegration of pre-Islamic religious patterns.

Muhammad, son of 'Abdallâh, was born in Mecca, the leading trading center of Northwestern Arabia, about the year 570 of the Christian era. He came from an impoverished branch of a noble clan—a social status characteristic of many a reformer.

Arabian paganism, which had never been systematized into a theology or pictorialized into a mythology, was already losing its hold over the minds of men. Whatever power it still commanded it owed, for the most part, to the traditionalism of the tribes whose very indifference in religious matters made for conservatism.

Both Judaism and Christianity were represented on the Arabian Peninsula. Within the memory of Muhammad's contemporaries, the Christian Abyssinians had annexed the Yemen, after crushing the indigenous dynasty that had adopted Judaism and, for a while at least, persecuted its Christian subjects. The Abyssinians tried to conquer Mecca, but failed and soon lost their foothold in Arabia to the Persians.

Mecca itself does not appear to have harbored an organized Jewish or Christian community of any size. The Jews, in the main members of Arab tribes won over by the Diaspora of the second century A.D., were concentrated in the oases of the North. Among the Christians, the hermits sufficiently impressed themselves on the Arabs' imagination to win mention in their poetry; but more numerous were foreigners and slaves who in Mecca formed a noticeable, though politically negligible, element of the lower strata of the population. These untaught Christians could convey scant doctrinal information, nor were the Jews of Mecca on a high enough level to transmit accurately the contents of the Torah. But both groups strengthened the latent trend toward monotheism and offered tools in the nature of simple tenets and illustrative legends toward that articulation of purer and more consistent beliefs which Muhammad felt it his mission to preach.

Islam is the last of the world religions originating in the lands east of the Mediterranean. Though closely akin to both Judaism and Christianity, it is an independent creation. Although its thought patterns are more closely related to Christianity—and indeed many generations of Christian theologians considered it but another heresy—Islamic practice, both ritual and legal, appears inspired rather by Judaism. The Jewish idea of the good life, organized to its least relevant detail in accordance with the rulings of Revelation, as interpreted by competent authorities, determined what the Muslim expected of his religion.

The basic beliefs of Islam are few and simple. As late as the twelfth century Averroes (d. 1198), the great philosopher who was to be so much more effective in the West than in the East, maintained that no one who accepted the oneness of God, His self-revelation through prophecy, and the Judgment of the Last Day could be charged with unbelief. The brief creed, *shahâda* (literally: testimony), which every Muslim is supposed to pronounce at least once, does not go beyond the twin statement: I bear witness that there is no god but God, *lâ ilâha illâ Allâh*, and that Muhammad is the messenger of God. The *shahâda* is the first of the five so-called *arkân*, or pillars, of the faith and, characteristically enough, the only one of doctrinal import. It is followed by *salât*, (ritual) prayer; *saum*, fasting (in the month of Ramadân); and *hajj*, the pilgrimage to the central sanctuary in Mecca.

It had been in the year 610 A.D. that Muhammad, a respected citizen, well-to-do, and through his marriage with Khadîja the head of a merchant house, received his first revelation. In the loneliness of Mount Hirâ, to which he had been accustomed to retreat for meditation, the Angel Gabriel appeared to him and told him—

Recite in the name of Thy Lord Who created,
Created man from clotted blood.
Recite, for Thy Lord is the most generous,
Who taught by the pen,
Taught man what he did not know (Koran 96:1-5).

After a period of anguish and uncertainty Muhammad found himself encouraged—

Rise and warn,
Thy Lord magnify
Thy garments purify,
The Wrath flee,
Bestow not favor to gain many,
For Thy Lord wait patiently (Koran 74:2-7).

The chain of revelations was to be broken only by Muhammad's death.

It was fear that motivated the Prophet: Fear of the impending end of this world, fear of the Judgment that would follow it and the punishment that would inevitably be meted out to the heedless. In days gone by, the Lord had sent bearers of warning to many a people to awaken them to the realization that nothing could save them but repentance to the One God, the Creator, Sustainer and Judge. Muhammad knew himself to be the end of a long line of messengers, fighters, and often martyrs of monotheism, bearers of the same truth phrased in their several tongues. What Moses had done for the Jews and Jesus for the Christians, he was to do for the Arabs. There would be no prophet after him. Time was running short. God was disposed to forgive the believer, to reward obedience to Himself and His messenger, but it was for man to win his rescue by allowing himself to be convinced by the miracle of Revelation, and by the uniqueness of the words which the Lord addressed to him. Commenting upon the Koran, the Lord said: *Verily if men and jinn agree to produce the like of this Koran, they will not produce the like of it though one to the other were backer* (Koran 17:90).

The earlier prophets had had to contend with scepticism and mockery, at times with violence. In picturing their plight Muhammad unveils his own difficulties and at the same time uses the typical sequence of events as added proof of his veracity. The sensitivity of the Meccans to his attacks on their local deities may have been keener than has been assumed. Yet they, as the Arabs in general, were familiar with the concept of a supreme god Allâh, of indistinct functions and character and without a cult, and there would not have been any real objection to Muhammad's endeavors to emphasize and clarify Allâh's role. Since the Meccans were free from apprehensions concerning the end of the world, the Last Judgment, and punishment after death, the shrill exhortations of the Prophet must have seemed incongruous, and perhaps even scurrilous.

The mainspring of their opposition, however, was social and economic. As Muhammad organized his followers, who were at first recruited mostly among the aliens and the dispossessed, into an "inter-tribal" community, they anticipated a threat to the structure of tribal society. The mere possibility of a conflict of loyalties was dangerous. Their city had grown around a tract of land considered sacred by a large section of the Arab tribes. To the local clans whose confederation actually controlled the informal "republic," its role as a mercantile center seemed inseparable from its religious role.

It was not until after Muhammad's *hijra* to Medina, an oasis two hundred miles to the north, where he had been invited to make peace between two Arab tribes, that he succeeded in consolidating his community. The significance of this "emigration" was so obvious that, soon after the Prophet's death, the year of the *hijra*, 622 A.D. was chosen as the first year of the Muhammadan era.

The rejection by the Jews of Medina of Muhammad's preaching led to their elimination in the sphere of politics. In theology the assertion was that the Jews and Christians had falsified their scriptures and that Islam constituted a return to the uncontaminated religion of Abraham, represented as the founder of the Ka'ba, the sanctuary of Mecca. By the substitution of the Ka'ba for Jerusalem as the *qibla*, the direction in which the worshipers face at prayer, the move toward greater independence from the Judaeo-Christian tradition was given visible expression. It was only in those early Medinan years that Islam identified itself with what we might loosely call Arab nationalism and pledged itself, not only to the conquest of Mecca, but also to the continuation of the essential (that is, in Muhammad's eyes—"pre-pagan," Abrahamitic) elements of the Arab heritage. Two years before Muhammad's death, in 630, Mecca surrendered after a token struggle.

The Revelation, which in Mecca had been primarily concerned with the Last Day, the fundamentals of theology and the tales of the earlier prophets, had in Medina come to include a great deal of political and legislative matter. The records of the Revelation were collected after the Prophet's death to form what is known as the *Qur'ân* (Koran), literally, "Reading." A government commission arranged the individual revelations, usually relatively short pieces, in 114 larger units, or *sûra's*, that follow each other generally in order of length. The opening *sûra*, the *Fâtiha*, is a short prayer, the last two are magic-religious invocations against evil.

The peculiar organization of the Book makes it difficult for the non-Muslim to derive much enjoyment from reading the Koran from cover to cover. Nor will he be able to realize the singular advance its style represents over anything pre-Islamic prose had to offer, although he cannot fail to be struck by the beauty of many of its passages. The Muslim who knows it to be the direct word of God realizes in the Koran his supreme experience of linguistic and oratorical perfection.

Faith and correct behavior will protect the Muslim from the Fire. Popular feeling has accepted the co-existence of two contradictory positions in Islam without finding it necessary to reconcile them on the intellectual plane. Although no expression is strong enough to depict the omnipotence of the Lord who is not bound by any law, physical or moral, and although man's fate unfolds as preordained, Allâh will not subject any believer to eternal punishment, perhaps because of His readiness to yield to the Prophet's intercession or perhaps simply in virtue of the believer's membership in the Muslim community.

As time wore on, the emphasis of piety shifted to some extent from God's majesty to His love, but to the simplehearted a certain reckless grandeur has remained the most impressive feature of that divinity which the Koran thus portrays in the much quoted Verse of the Throne:

God—there is no god but He, the Living, the Eternal; slumber seizes Him not, nor sleep; to Him belongs whatever is in the heavens and whatever is in the earth. Who is there that shall intercede with Him except by His permission? He knoweth what is before them and what is behind them, and they comprehend not anything of His knowledge but what He willeth. His throne is wide as the heavens and the earth, to guard them wearieth Him not. He is the Exalted, the Mighty (Koran 2:256).

Correct behavior includes the regular performance of the prayer ritual. The formalized prayer, *salât*, consists of a sequence of movements accompanied by the pronunciation of certain formulae, some of which are brief Koranic texts. The *mu'adhdhin* (muezzin), sounds the *adhân*, the call to prayer—there are no bells nor clappers, such as are used by Eastern Christians, in the mosque. The believer is free to pray by himself, but joining the congregation in the mosque (*masjid*, "place of prostration") is preferred.

Here the believers, facing toward Mecca, range themselves in rows behind a prayer leader, *imâm*, who is generally paid for his services from the mosque's endowment fund, but who is in no way a cleric. In fact, any Muslim possessed of the necessary technical knowledge may act as *imâm*. The originally prescribed two prayers were soon, under the influence of Jewish and perhaps also Zoroastrian custom, increased to five. They are of unequal length—the prayer at daybreak consisting of two *rak'a*, or "bowings"; the noon and midafternoon prayers of four each; the prayer after sunset of three; and that of the early part of the night again of four.

Each *rak'a* consists "of seven movements with their appropriate recitations: (1) the recitation of the phrase *Allâhu akbar*, "God is most great," with the hands open on each side of the face; (2) the recitation of the *Fâtiha*, followed by another passage or passages from the Koran, while standing upright; (3) bowing from the hips; (4) straightening up; (5) sliding to the knees and a first prostration with face to the ground; (6) sitting back on the haunches; (7) a second prostration. The second and later 'bowings' begin with the second of these movements, and at the end of each pair of 'bowings' and the conclusion of the whole prayer the worshipper recites the *shahâda* and the ritual salutations." [1]

Only after his ritual obligations have been defrayed is the believer permitted, and even encouraged, to address a personal invocation, *du'â'*, to his Lord. Since prayer is valid only when performed in a state of ritual purity, it has to be preceded by ablution, *wudû'*. *When ye stand up for the Prayer*, the Koran ordains, *wash your faces and your hands up to the elbows, and wipe your heads and your feet up to the ankles; . . . If ye be sick or on a journey, . . . and do not find water, sand yourselves with dry good sand, and rub your faces and your hands with it; Allâh doth not wish to place upon you any difficulty, but He wishes to purify and to complete His goodness towards you; mayhap ye will show thankfulness* (Koran 5:8-9). It is the duty of ablution before *salât* that accounts for the presence of fountains in the mosque courts.

In imitation of, and in contrast with, the Jewish and the Christian forms of the Sabbath institution, Muhammad appointed Friday as the day of a solemnized community prayer. This takes the place of the ordinary noon service. *O ye who have believed, when proclamation is made for the Prayer on the day of the assembly* [Friday] *endeavor to come to the remembrance of Allâh, and leave off bargaining; that is better for you, if ye have knowledge.— Then when the Prayer is finished, scatter abroad in the land and seek the bounty of Allâh, but call Allâh frequently to mind; mayhap ye will prosper* (Koran 62:9-10). In other words, Friday is not to be a day of rest, and business is to be suspended only during the noon-service itself.

This service is shortened to two *rak'a* as against the four of the regular noon-prayer (which remains obligatory for him who misses the community prayer), but is enriched by the so-called *khutba*, an address or sermon. The *khutba* is not, however, as Christian or Jewish analogies might lead one to expect, a discussion of a religious question or the application of religious principle to a problem of the day. Its content is fixed—in addition to the praise of God and a blessing of the Prophet, it must offer a prayer for the Muslim community, a recitation from the Koran and an admonition to piety. Furthermore, God's blessing will be invoked on the head of the state; in fact, the mention of his name in the Friday *khutba* and its appearance on the coinage are in Muslim law the two foremost symbols of sovereignty.

Muslim ritual crystallized too early to be significantly affected by religious and cultural trends developing within Islam as a consequence of its rise to power over erstwhile Byzantine and Persian territories. The formalistic bent of mind of the canon lawyers whom the community, despite some protests, was inclined to accept as the guardians of the faith almost completely prevented variation or change of the liturgy. Muhammad was quoted as having said: "The prescribed worship is like a balance: whoever pays is repaid in full." [2] Thus participation in the liturgy would strengthen the believer's confidence in his ultimate reward. It also would strengthen his feeling of being part of the well-ordered community of the elect, but the mechanistic conception of prayer made valid through mere form would often fail to evoke a specifically religious experience.

There were some, however, for whom communication with the Lord was not impaired by the rigidity of the ceremonial, like the worshiper of whom it was told that, when he was about to pray, his hair stood on end and he trembled and said: "The hour has come to fulfil a trust which the heavens and the earth were unable to bear." [3] But for others the significance of the prescribed gesture had to be elaborated by symbolic or moralistic interpretation. Thus the great teacher and theologian Ghazzâlî (d. 1111) explains in his discussion of prayer: "Next you bend down for the prostration, which is the highest degree of submission, for the dearest of your members, which is your face, gets hold of the humblest thing, which is the dust. . . . Whenever you place your self in the place of lowliness, know that you have placed it in its proper place and have returned the branch to the trunk, for of the dust were you formed and to it you return." [4]

Emphasis was laid on the "inward stipulations"—humility and an attending heart. Purification is understood as purification from lust; the turning toward the *qibla*, as facing the Throne of God, that is, becoming absorbed in the mystery of Divine contemplation. One of the mystics said: "Four things are necessary to him who prays: annihilation of the lower soul, loss of the natural powers, purity of the inmost heart, and perfect contemplation." Annihilation of the lower soul, the author goes on to say, is to be attained only by concentration of thought; loss of the natural powers only by affirmation of the Divine majesty . . . ; purity of the inmost heart only by love; and perfect contemplation only by purity of the inmost heart.

Another mystic reports: "In my boyhood I remember seeing a female ascetic who was bitten by a scorpion in forty places while she was praying, but no change of expression was visible in her countenance. When she had finished, I said: 'O mother, why didst thou not fling the scorpion away from thee?' She answered: 'Ignorant boy! dost thou deem it right that while I am engaged in God's business I should attend to my own?' " [5]

As there is no Muslim celebration devoid of religious context, there is none without prayer and its peculiar formalism. And as to prayer itself, the celebrant is able to give meaning to ceremony and festival on several levels of sublimation or interpretation. The believer's experience might range from a near-pagan response to the sacred action to its symbolic attenuation in mystical allegory. It may be conditioned by Bedouin simplicity or by the emotional sophistication of the Hellenized philosopher. The law demands the act. God only scrutinizes the hearts. But He may be counted on to be lenient, for has He not ruled that deeds should be judged by their intentions?

★

ii . *Pilgrimage*

IT WAS PROBABLY THREE OR FOUR YEARS after the *hijra* that the following revelation came to the Prophet:

The first house founded for the people was that at Bakka [Mecca], *a blessed house and a guidance to the worlds.—In it are signs, evidences—the station of Abraham, and the security of him who enters it; pilgrimage to the house is due to Allâh from the people, whoever is able to make his way thither.—But if anyone disbelieves, Allâh is rich beyond need of the worlds* (Koran 3:90-92).

In due course this injunction was developed into the fifth "pillar" of Islam—the obligatory Pilgrimage to Mecca, 'Arafa and Minà,—and in a sense the culmination of the believer's religious experience. Once in his lifetime every Muslim, man or woman, must journey to these Holy Places to participate at a given time in a given sequence of ceremonial actions. A mere visit or the performance of the rites at a different season would not constitute a fulfillment of this duty and would leave him, as the Prophet is quoted as having said, "to die as a Jew or a Christian."

The canon lawyers have bestowed a great deal of attention on defining the "ability" to make the Pilgrimage, the absence of which according to the Koranic passage automatically exempts the individual believer from carrying out the order addressed to the community. There is general agreement that the obligation does not apply to the unfree and the insane. Minors, too, are exempt, and so are women unable to travel with their husbands or relatives within the forbidden degrees, that is, relatives with whom marriage is forbidden. Some controversy attaches to the material means the Muslim must possess before starting on the *hajj*. Most authorities disapprove of a pilgrim's begging his way to Mecca—a stipulation which is, however, frequently disregarded, especially by African pilgrims. Insecurity of the roads and the impossibility to procure suitable land transportation are also recognized as legitimate reasons for postponement.

On the other hand, delays when circumstances are favorable are frowned upon, and only one of the four predominant law schools allows the Pilgrimage to be carried out in the name, and for the spiritual benefit, of a deceased person by whose estate the expenses of the substitute pilgrim (who does not derive any religious advantage from his journey) are defrayed. In practice, then, the decision whether or not to undertake the Pilgrimage is left more or less to the individual. And it is obvious that at no period more than a small fraction of the Muslim community (which may at present number some 270 million adherents) could have taken part in the *hajj*. On the other hand, a sizable fraction of the pilgrims appear to have returned to Mecca to repeat it—an action not required, but highly meritorious.

The inclusion of the Pilgrimage among the duties of the faithful implied the selection of Mecca as the spiritual center of the new religion and put the contemporaries on notice that the Muslims meant to gain control of the city. It could be interpreted as a declaration that the new religion and the Arab tradition were not incompatible. It is interesting to observe that Muhammad developed the idea of the Pilgrimage in some detail at a time when his political situation as the head of a community of exiles must have seemed to deprive his declarations of any practical significance.

Renewed revelations fairly quickly accustomed the Muslims to the function within Islam of the Meccan sanctuary. *When We* [i.e., God] *appointed the House* [in

1. The *Masjid al-Haram*, Mecca.

From A. J. B. Wavell, *A Modern Pilgrim in Mecca and a Siege in Sanaa*, London, 1913. By permission of publisher, Constable & Co., Ltd.

2. Muhammad with 'Alî and other companions at the Ka'ba.

"The faces of Muhammad [on the camel] and of 'Alî are covered with veils, out of religious awe. The locale is rendered with a view to show everything as clearly as possible and certain parts are therefore painted in bird's eye view, others in profile. This approach was first used in tomb scenes of Ancient Egypt." Dr. Richard Ettinghausen; quoted by permission.

From an Indian manuscript, dated 1761. (Berlin, Ethnographic Museum.)

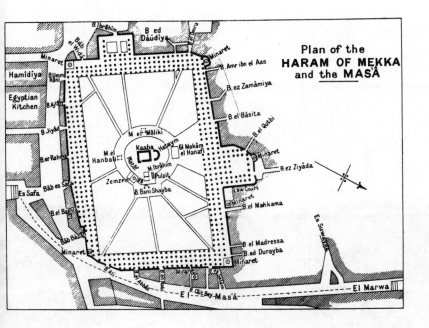

3. Plan of the *Haram* of Mecca and the *Mas'â*.

From E. Rutter, *The Holy Cities of Arabia*, London and New York, 1928, G. P. Putnam's Sons.

4. The *Haram* with the Ka'ba from the northeast.

To the left of the Ka'ba the *hatîm* is clearly visible. The marble pavement surrounding the House is the *matâf*. Immediately in front of the House is the *Maqâm Ibrâhîm* and behind it the *Bâb Banî Shaiba*. To the right of the *Bâb* is the well-house of the Zamzam. The Black Stone is embedded in the corner closest to the spectator.

From Ibrâhîm Rif'at Pasha, *Mir'ât al-haramain*, Cairo, 1344/1925.

Mecca] *to be a place of resort and a security for the people . . . and We covenanted with Abraham and Ishmael: "Purify My House for those who circle around it, and for those who cleave to it, and for those who bow and prostrate themselves"* (Koran 2:119). Having thus proclaimed the pre-pagan character of the Meccan rites and claimed them for the Muslims, Muhammad, strengthened by the Meccans' failure to conquer Medina, went one step further. *Verily those who have disbelieved and turn others aside from the way of Allâh, and from the Sacred Mosque which we have appointed for the people, equally for those continually about it and for the stranger* [that is, as a central, not a local temple], *whoever wills in regard to it diversion from its purpose wrongously, we shall give to taste of punishment painful* (Koran 22:25-26).

When Mecca had fallen the Prophet did not, however, hasten to perform the Pilgrimage in person. Instead he sent his father-in-law, Abû Bakr—who was soon to succeed him as the leader of the state—to lead the faithful. Muhammad had his son-in-law, 'Alî—destined to be his fourth successor, or caliph—read this revelation to the pilgrims foregathered in 'Arafa:

Renunciation by Allâh and His messenger of the polytheists with whom ye have made covenants . . . and a proclamation from Allâh and His messenger to the people on the day of the greatest pilgrimage, that Allâh renounces the polytheists, [as does] also His messenger. . . . It is not for the polytheists to visit Allâh's place of worship, giving evidence of unbelief against themselves; the works of such are of no avail, and in the Fire they abide.—They only shall visit Allâh's places of worship who have believed in Allâh and the Last Day, have established the Prayer and paid the Poor-Tax, and have feared nothing but Allâh; possibly such will be among those who are rightly guided (Koran 9:1. 3a. 17-18).

It is on the basis of these lines that to this very day non-Muslims are forbidden, not only to view or share in the Pilgrimage itself, but to visit Mecca even outside the season of the *hajj*. Westerners have been unable to enter Mecca, except as *bona fide* Muslims or in disguise.

Only after these preparatory steps had been taken did the Prophet himself set out on the Pilgrimage. This *hajjat al-wadâ'*—The Farewell Pilgrimage, as it came to be called after Muhammad died, less than three months after his return to Medina (d. June 8, 632)—was intended to become the model for all future celebrations of the festival. A huge body of tradition has sprung up describing the Prophet's behavior down to the most insignificant detail. Whenever in later times doubts arose as to the correct execution of some fine point of the ceremonial, the prophetic precedent or a pious fiction invested with Muhammad's authority was cited to resolve the difficulty. The regulation of the Pilgrimage completed Muhammad's work—only then did the faithful know how their God wished to be served. *Today I have perfected your religion for you, and have completed My goodness towards you, and have approved Islam as your religion* (Koran 5:5).

On the intellectual level the immediate consequence of Muhammad's choice of Mecca for his religious capital—unlike Jerusalem and Rome, it was never to be the political center of the believers—was the development of two ideological cycles, which in their justification and dramatization of Mecca's religious function still continue to color the Muslim's experience of the *hajj*. The legends clustering about the Koranic passage, [Remember] *when Abraham raised the foundations of the House along with Ishmael . . .* (Koran 2:121), are demonstrably not elaborations of local pagan themes, but are of recent, that is, Islamic origin. Their tendency and their style are typical of Muslim legends in general—no detail must be allowed to go unexplained or unnamed and the action as a whole must be tied in with the traditional sequence of sacred history.

There is no agreement whether Abraham or Ibrâhîm, to give the name its Arabic form, was commanded to erect the Ka'ba (literally: cube) before or after he had cast out

Hagar. In any case, the place where he was to build was indicated to him in a miraculous manner. The stones of the Ka'ba were quarried in three of the mountains overlooking Mecca, Mount Hermon (the Lebanon) and the Mount of Olives. When the walls had reached a certain height, Ibrâhîm stepped on a stone which still shows the imprint of his feet, the so-called Maqâm Ibrâhîm—the Station of Abraham. Upon completion of the work, Abraham again mounted the Maqâm that then towered over the mountains and proclaimed to all mankind the obligation to make the Pilgrimage. The Black Stone, which forms part of the eastern corner of the building and is of extraordinary holiness, was brought down to Abraham by Gabriel (who later was to transmit the word of the Lord to Muhammad). At that time the stone was white and it turned black only because of its contact with the sin and impurity of the pagan period.

Another version carries the foundation of the Ka'ba beyond Abraham and represents Adam in the role of its builder. Originally, it is said, Adam was so tall he could listen to the song of the Heavenly Host about the Throne of the Lord. Due to his fall, he shrank and no longer reached into the celestial spheres. To comfort him, God sent down to Mecca, where Adam had gone after his expulsion from Paradise, a tent which he was to circumambulate even as the angels move around the Throne. But Mecca was without inhabitants and the sanctuary without worshipers. So God promised to Adam that Mecca was to harbor a cult of especial sanctity and blessing.

A variant specifies that the tent was made of red hyacinth —a curious reflection of the *qubba*, the red leather tent in which the tribal chieftain of the pagan period would keep the tribal idol next to his own. Adam lived in the red tent, using a white hyacinth (that was later to become the Black Stone) as his seat. When God made His covenant with mankind, in which they recognized His dominion, He had the Stone swallow the document. On Judgment Day the Stone will be endowed with a tongue to bear witness against mankind.

The second cycle was to account for the selection of Mecca as the location of the Ka'ba. It did so by assigning Mecca a special cosmological function, or more exactly, by transferring to Mecca cosmological ideas in vogue among Jews and Christians concerning the sanctuary of Jerusalem. The sanctuary is conceived of as the navel of the earth. It was created before the rest of the earth. "Forty years or according to others, two thousand years, before Allâh created the heavens and earth, the Ka'ba was a dry spot floating on the water and from it the world has been spread out." [1] It is argued that this is the reason why the Koran refers to Mecca as the Mother of Towns, which is interpreted in a geographical sense to be the center of the earth.

The navel, however, is not only the highest point on earth, but also the "place of communication with the upper and the nether world." Tradition duly asserts that at Mecca heaven is nearest to the earth and a story is told that implies that prayers are more easily heard in Mecca because of its connection with heaven. The *bi'r*, well or pit, reported to have been situated within the Ka'ba in heathen times, which served for offerings to be thrown down, was in all likelihood meant as the contact point with the nether world.

Moreover, Mecca itself is described as a sepulcher. Adam is said to be buried in Mecca and it is even reported to harbor the tomb of Muhammad—in the face of the well-known fact that the Prophet's grave-cupola in Medina was shortly after his death on the way to becoming the goal of pilgrims. But not only Adam and Muhammad, scores and hundreds of prophets are believed to rest in Mecca. In fact, "Every prophet, after his people had perished, would establish himself at Mecca; there, he and his followers with him, used to perform worship till he died." Mecca, as the center of the earth, is the natural place of origin of any prophet and, therefore, in the logic of the legends, also the place where he must meet his end.

But the Ka'ba is not only the center of the earth, it is the center of the universe. The Koran speaks of seven heavens and seven earths, which are thought of as superimposed one upon the other. Every heaven and every earth has its center marked by a sanctuary as its navel and "the imaginary axis of the Universe runs through fourteen sanctuaries." The highest of them is the Throne of God. At each of them the same ceremonies are carried out that are carried out at the Ka'ba. So the sanctuary of Mecca is established as the religious center of the universe and the cosmic significance of any ritual act performed there is clearly demonstrated. By explaining that "the origin of the clay of the messenger of God is from the navel of the earth in Mecca, the person of the Prophet is integrated in this system of universal worship."

Mecca, the chief town of the Hijâz and at present inhabited by perhaps 60,000 to 70,000 people, was known to Ptolemy (second century A.D.) as Makoraba, the South Arabic and Ethiopian *mikrâb*, meaning the temple. The settlement was located at the intersection of the frankincense road on which goods from the East reached the Mediterranean, with highways leading from Mesopotamia to the Red Sea at Jidda, just forty-five miles to the west. It owed its existence to the Well Zamzam, the only source of water in the barren north to south valley, of which the historical city takes up a basin of some two miles in length and half a mile in width. The mountains to the west, varying in height from 1,500 to 3,000 feet, keep the valley (about 400 feet) from being properly ventilated.

The Koran (14:40) introduces Abraham as saying: *O our Lord, I have caused some of my descendants to dwell in a valley where there is no sown land, beside Thy sacred house* . . . and the contrast between the sterility of the city and its immediate surroundings and the rich vegetation in the highlands beyond has been observed by many an Arab geographer. In 966, Maqdisî complains of its "suffocating heat, deadly winds, clouds of flies." [2]

The city as it was constituted in Muhammad's day has been called "a merchant republic" [3] and the Koran (106:2) makes reference *to the double caravan of winter and summer* and continues (106:3–4) with the exhortation: *So let them serve the Lord of this House* [the Ka'ba] *Who feeds them against hunger and makes them safe against fear*, thus uniting in a single passage the two sources of livelihood of the town—commerce and the pilgrim trade. Not much has changed since that time, except that the pilgrims have increasingly become the mainspring of Meccan prosperity.

At the time of the Prophet, the tribe of Quraish held the town, occupying mainly its central hollow with the Zamzam and Ka'ba. Today the only survivors of the Prophet's clansmen are the Sharîfs who ruled Mecca until, in 1924, it passed under the control of Ibn Saud, and the Banû Shaiba who from time immemorial have held the keys to the Ka'ba.

The Swiss explorer, John Lewis Burckhardt (d. 1817), who visited Mecca in 1814 and who still seems to be the Western traveler most highly esteemed by the Muslims,[4] called it "a handsome town: its streets are in general broader than those of eastern cities; the houses lofty, and built of stone; and the numerous windows that face the streets give them a more lively and European aspect than those of Egypt and Syria, where the houses present but few windows toward the exterior. Mekka (like Djidda) contains many houses three stories high; few at Mekka are white-washed; but the dark grey colour of the stone is much preferable to the glaring white that offends the eyes in Djidda." [5]

At about the middle of the town's principal axis, the street widens to a large courtyard and colonnades accessible through nineteen gates, the *Masjid al-Harâm* or Great Mosque, that has grown around the Ka'ba and Zamzam. The dimensions of the *Harâm*, inside the colonnades—northwest side, 545 feet; southeast side, 554; northeast side, 360; southwest side, 364 feet [6]—characterize it as a somewhat irregular parallelogram. It has been estimated that 35,000 worshipers can assemble in the area. Almost exactly in the middle stands the Ka'ba. It is an irregular cube, measuring "some 40 feet in length by 33 feet in breadth," and no two of its sides are exactly alike in length. The height, as E. Rutter describes it, "including the topmost part of the walls, which forms a parapet round the edge of the roof, is some 50 feet. It is firmly and massively built of the fine Mekkan granite, while the roof, which is sunk a distance of 2½ or 3 feet below the top of the walls, is of a greyish-white marble. The foundations of the Ka'ba are reinforced by a sloping bulwark of marble" ten inches high, projecting about a foot, the so-called *shâdharwân*. There is but one door which is situated in the northeastern wall, about seven feet above the ground to protect the interior from being flooded. On the relatively rare occasions when the Ka'ba is opened—usage varies, but some ten times a year on the average, not counting the three solemn washings of the interior—a wooden staircase running on wheels is placed against the door. The interior is unfurnished except for numerous gold and silver lamps suspended from the ceiling, which is supported by three wooden pillars.

The Black Stone, variously described as lava, basalt and an aerolite, and actually of a dark red-brown color, is built into the eastern corner, about five feet above ground. Split in a conflagration, it now consists of three large and several small pieces tied together by a silver band. Its diameter is estimated at twelve inches. The Black Stone is kissed by the believers when they circumambulate the Ka'ba—a survival of the original stone cult whose approbation by the Prophet disquieted some of his followers. One of them, the future Caliph 'Umar, is quoted as saying: "Verily I know that thou art but a stone. Thou canst do no harm, neither canst thou confer advantage. And had I not seen God's Messenger kiss thee, neither would I have kissed thee." In 1932, an Afghan pilgrim who had broken off a fragment of the stone was executed, and the piece was refitted by King Ibn Saud himself.[7]

The space of approximately six feet between the eastern corner and the door, the *multazam*, is of special sanctity and it is there that the devout press their breasts and outstretched arms against the wall to become impregnated with the *baraka*, the blessing or virtue, that is immanent in the holy building. The section of the northwest wall between the gilt waterspout, the *mîzâb ar-rahma*, or Water-spout of Mercy, and the west corner is the exact *qibla*. The walls of the Ka'ba have since pre-Islamic times been covered with a curtain, at first of striped cloth but now of black brocade—the *kiswa*, into which the *shahâda* is woven. The *kiswa* is generally provided by the Egyptian government at an expense of some eighteen to twenty thousand dollars. It is changed every year and sold in small pieces to the pilgrims. It will be recalled that the Jewish Tabernacle, the High Places of Canaan, the Throne of Solomon as well as the sacred tents of pagan Arabia and the fabulous Lotus at the Boundary in Paradise (Koran 52:14) are all covered with cloth.[8]

A few steps from the southeast corner of the Ka'ba is the domed building (in its present form dating from 1661) that covers the Well of Zamzam, a shaft of some 130 feet in depth, which possesses the miraculous property that its level will never fall, however much of its water the pilgrims may have used. It was opened by Gabriel to save Hagar and Ishmael from dying of thirst. The slightly brackish water is believed to be of infallible curative value and the pilgrims, in addition to dipping their shrouds into it, usually take home some bottles as presents for application in illness or for ablution after death. The distribution of the water is in the hands of the *Zamzamî*, a more or less hereditary guild.

Between the northeastern wall of the Ka'ba and the Bâb Banî Shaiba, an arch through which one enters on the *matâf* or the oval pavement of about 150 by 125 feet on which the circumambulation of the Ka'ba is performed, stands the small dome of the Maqâm Ibrâhîm. A depression in the *matâf* facing the door is called "the trough" and believed to be the place where Abraham and Ishmael mixed the mortar they used in building the Ka'ba. Between the Ka'ba's northwest wall and a low semicircular wall, the *hatîm*, up to which the sanctuary reached at one time, in the so-called *hijr*, are the graves of Ishmael and his mother Hagar. The only other conspicuous, though small, buildings in the courtyard are the *maqâms* from which the prayer-leaders of the several ritual schools direct the *salât*. No major changes in the architecture of the *Harâm* have been made since the Turkish Sultan Selim II, between 1572 and 1577, replaced the roofs of the colonnades by a number of cone-shaped domes.[9]

When the Prophet conquered Mecca, he had the stone idols that stood around the Ka'ba destroyed. These are said to have numbered 360—a figure characteristic of an astral cult. Muhammad also smashed the wooden figure of a dove, the sacred bird of the goddess of love. In this connection, the innumerable doves that live in the Mosque without, according to report, ever soiling the roof of the Ka'ba require mention. Like every Semitic sanctuary, the Ka'ba made the surrounding area into consecrated ground—*haram*. The sacred territory, which spreads beyond the limits of the town proper, was a place of truce and asylum for man and beast. Except for certain noxious kinds, no animal was to be killed there, no criminal executed, not even a shrub cut down. Islam has perpetuated these regulations.

What is the effect of the Great Mosque on the visitor? A British traveler, who saw it in 1908, avers that "the outstanding impression . . . is that of the unusual. It is not beautiful, it could not fairly be called majestic, but it awes one by its strangeness. One feels instinctively that one is looking on something unique. . . ."[10] The reaction of the famous North African traveler, Ibn Battûta (d. 1377), is somewhat similar, although, of course, considerably more emphatic: "The most magnificent Ka'ba stands in the midst of the Great Mosque. Its appearance is so singular and its sight so pleasing that no tongue can adequately depict its extraordinary features nor any description encompass the beauty of its perfection."

Batanûnî, an Egyptian official, who went to Mecca in 1909, observes: "It is strange that everyone whose eye falls on the Ka'ba for the first time will be seen to be profoundly disturbed not because his eye has fallen on something unwonted but because of the fear and awe that overwhelm him. You will see those onlookers shaken to the bones because of the reverence-inspiring sight. Some halt for a moment in front of this supreme grandeur in the attitude of a well-disciplined, humble person who is aware of his own insignificance; others shout with a frightened voice while their tongue forms disconnected words; others again fight their tears and you hear from them no sound but a weeping that chokes their voice and breaks up their breathing. And with everyone of them the fear of God is proportionate to the strength of his religion and the firmness of his faith." [11]

Mecca must be entered in a state of consecration, *ihrâm*. With the exception of people such as camel-drivers whose profession compels them to enter the town at frequent intervals, every visitor to the sacred territory must acquit himself of either the *hajj* or the *'umra*, the so-called "Little Pilgrimage" which is not bound to any particular time of the year, or of both. At some point of his journey he has to leave the sphere of the profane. He may do so upon departing from his home or anywhere en route, but at the latest at one of the *mîqât*, or "stations," which custom has marked out on each of the main roads to Mecca some distance outside the *haram*. Pilgrims arriving by sea will take the *ihrâm* when their boat has reached a point off the nearest *mîqât* on land or else will consecrate themselves at Jidda.

Pilgrimage, like prayer, may be commenced only in a state of purity. So when the *hâjj*, or Mecca pilgrim, reaches his *mîqât* he first performs a complete ablution. In view of the ceremonial restrictions imposed on him while in a state of consecration, which include the prohibition of shaving, cutting or plucking one's hair, clipping one's nails, washing or anointing oneself, the pilgrim now lavishes great care on his toilet. He dresses in a garment that consists of two unsewn and preferably white sheets, also referred to as *ihrâm*—the *izâr*, which reaches from the navel to the knees, and the *ridâ'*, which is thrown around the body covering the left shoulder, back and breast, but leaving free part of the right arm. Any material will do; only silks and ornamented fabrics are prohibited. The head remains totally uncovered, but the use of an umbrella against the sun is permitted. The instep, too, must not be covered. The law does not prescribe any particular dress for women, but custom imposes the use of a long robe reaching from head to foot. A woman pilgrim conceals her face, which ought to be uncovered, by a mask that keeps the fabric from touching the skin. When it is considered that this array is the only covering to be worn for many a day and, strictly speaking, also at night, the extremely uncomfortable character of the *hajj* period will be realized.

The canon lawyers have concerned themselves with every conceivable infringement on the restrictions that are placed on the *muhrim* (the person in the state of *ihrâm*) and that includes the prohibition of bloodshed and uprooting of plants. All infringements may be atoned for by sacrifice or the distribution of wheat to the poor, with the lone exception of sexual relations, which result in rendering the Pilgrimage null and void. The analogy between *hajj* and *salât*, which is keenly felt by Muslim theologians, is emphasized by both being the only religious practices which require "consecration"—that is the complete severance of ties with the profane world. This transition from the secular to the consecrated state is effected in prayer by the initial *takbîr*, or exclamation of "God is most great," known as *takbîrat al-ihrâm*.

It is easy to see the connection of the behavior to be observed during *ihrâm* with ancient Semitic ritual. The dress, identical with the *hulla*, the shrouding garments of the pagan Arabs, and again with the dress of the gods,[12] is in all likelihood the sacred dress of the old Semites. The upper garment of the High Priest in the Old Testament was seamless. The *ephod* of the Jewish priests, worn around the hips, and the *me'îl*, worn around the shoulders, were white. The Jewish mourner, as well as the officiating priest, went barefooted. Nor may the Jewish mourner bathe or pare his nails. The mourning-women of pre-Islamic paganism are described as dirty and unkempt. As to the prohibition of cutting one's hair, which in a slightly different form is familiar to us through the Old Testament, it has been suggested that the *muḥrim* consecrates himself by devoting his hair, which is part of himself and may be taken to represent himself, as an offering at the sanctuary.

On the assumption of the *iḥrâm*, the *niyya* must be pronounced. Any devotional practice, and in particular prayer and Pilgrimage, is valid only when preceded by a declaration of "intention." So the pilgrim must state clearly that he has taken the *iḥrâm* as an act of duty to the Lord for the *ḥajj* (or the *'umra*, or both). Once placed under a certain "intention," the *iḥrâm* cannot be made to serve a different purpose. While a pilgrim is free to "intend" his *iḥrâm* at the outset for a combination of *'umra* and *ḥajj*, he can not, if his *niyya* or "intention" has been limited to a *ḥajj*, change it to include the lesser pilgrimage as well.

The formulation of the *niyya* is followed by the *talbiya* —the calling of *labbaika*, "At Thy service"—which is the essential sign of the consecrated state. It should be spoken clearly, but not shouted, for "He upon Whom it calls is neither deaf nor far away." The formula, the crucial words of which antedate Islam, allows of some variation, but usually runs as follows:

> *Here I am, O My God, here I am* (or: *At Thy Service, O Lord, at Thy Service; labbaika, Allâhumma, labbaika*);
> *No partner hast Thou, here am I;*
> *Verily the praise and the grace are Thine, and the empire—No partner hast Thou, here am I.*[13]

And, just as in the *salât* the *takbîr* is repeated at each new phase, so the pilgrim is expected to call out the *talbiya* at each phase of the *ḥajj*—when meeting another caravan, when mounting or descending a slope and when approaching the several sanctuaries of the pilgrimage. For the *mu'tamir*, the person who performs the *'umra*, the *talbiya* ceases no later than on reaching the Ka'ba. For the *ḥâjj* it continues almost to the end of the ceremonies, that is, until "desacralization" or the descent from the state of consecration starts.

As soon as possible after his arrival, the pilgrim enters the Great Mosque through the northern gate of the north-eastern colonnades—the Bâb as-Salâm, or Gate of Peace—passes through the arch of the Banî Shaiba toward the Black Stone and begins from there, keeping the Ka'ba to his left, seven circumambulations (*tawâf*) of the House. If he has intended to make the '*umra* (or '*umra* and *hajj*), the *tawâf* will form part of it. If he has set out only on the *hajj*, it will represent the "circumambulation of arrival" or "of salutation" which, although not an integral part of the pilgrimage, is recommended practice. It would seem that the *tawâf* was originally part of the '*umra* alone and that it was Muhammad himself who inserted it into the *hajj*. In any case, not only is the rite of walking or running around a stone, an altar, or a sanctuary of any kind attested by pre-Islamic poetry in which wild kine are likened to virgins circling an idol,[14] but it can be traced in Jewish ritual in which at one time during the Feast of Tabernacles the altar was circled once on each of the six first days and seven times on the seventh. And in more recent times sevenfold circumambulation has become connected with the tombs of certain Muslim saints.

In Mecca, the circumambulation has to be executed on the *matâf*—the *shâdharwân* (the marble reinforcement) must not be stepped on—and is sometimes done barefoot. The heathen custom of performing it in a state of nakedness was abolished by the Prophet. The first three circlings are done at a quickened pace, called *ramal*, with the *ridâ'* arranged in *idtibâ'*, that is, "passed beneath the right arm and the ends folded over the left shoulder—leaving the right arm and shoulder bare."[15] In passing, the Black Stone should be kissed or, if the crowd does not permit such close approach, it should be touched with hand or staff and the touch transferred to the face. Another stone built into the opposite corner should only be touched, but not kissed. All through the *tawâf* appropriate prayers must be recited. After the seventh circling, the visitor presses himself against the *multazam*. He then prays two *rak'a* at the Maqâm Ibrâhîm and drinks of the Zamzam water. The distance covered in executing the prescribed seven circuits amounts to about nine-tenths of a mile. The importance of the circumambulation is reflected in the fact that the original meaning of the root *hajj* is "to describe a circle"—in other words, the Pilgrimage received its name from this key rite.

The pilgrim now leaves the Mosque, left foot forward, through the Bâb as-Safâ, in the southeast colonnades, from which a small lane leads to the *Mas'à*, or "place of running." This is a relatively wide street and one of the principal markets of the city. It starts at a small, paved platform approached by some steps—the hill of as-Safâ. Here the pilgrim turns to the Ka'ba, which is not visible from this point, and says a prayer. He then descends the *Mas'à*, which passes around the southeastern corner of the *Haram*. Built into the Mosque wall which overlooks the *Mas'à* at this point is a stone pillar, faced by a similar pillar on the opposite side of the way. Both are painted green and have been so for at least seven centuries. About six paces before he reaches them, the pilgrim breaks into a run, *harwal*, which he keeps up for some eighty yards at the end of which he passes two more such marks. He then proceeds at his usual pace to the end of the *Mas'à*, which here becomes another small hill called al-Marwa, with a platform somewhat higher than that of as-Safâ. After an invocation, the pilgrim returns to as-Safâ. The *Mas'à* must be traversed altogether seven times, a total distance of not quite two miles.

The *sa'y*, or "running," ends at al-Marwa, where the *mu'tamir* has his hair cut and is therewith "desacralized." The *hâjj*, on the other hand, has only a token clipping done to him, since he is to continue in a state of consecration to the end of the Pilgrimage. Contrary to the *tawâf*, which is a meritorious practice in its own right, the *sa'y* is not an independent rite. Originally, the running seems to have taken place between two idols, Isâf and Nâ'ila. The later Muslim tradition records that Adam and Eve once rested for a while on the two hills. Another legend portrays Hagar as running seven times between Safâ and Marwa to look for water when Ishmael was dying of thirst. The *harwal* is explained as a reminiscence of Abraham's attempt to escape Satan who had hid himself in the valley to ambush him.

The two processions, *tawâf* and *sa'y*, were originally independent ceremonies which were combined for the sake of unifying all cults attached to Meccan localities. This unification was done with a view to connecting them with the sanctuary that had been given central importance by Islam—the Ka'ba. The Koran makes it clear that the *sa'y* is a rite that does not really belong to the *'umra: Safâ and Marwa are among the manifestations of Allâh, so if anyone performs the pilgrimage to the House or the 'umra, it is no fault in him that he makes the circuit of them; if one does good spontaneously, Allâh is grateful, knowing* (Koran 2:153). It is in the same spirit that Islam welded the procession around the Ka'ba and the age-old Pilgrimage to 'Arafa (or 'Arafât) into the comprehensive celebration of the *hajj*.

The *hajj* proper begins on the eighth of Dhu 'l-Hijja, the last month of the Muslim year. On the seventh, the pilgrims listen to an address at the Ka'ba which rehearses the ceremonies they are about to go through. On the next day they move along the eastern road to the village of Minà (today mostly pronounced Munà) situated in a narrow valley, hemmed in by steep and completely barren rocks which are overtowered on the north by Mount Thabîr. Except for a few stately houses, Minà is a settlement of shops and khans and lies deserted throughout the year but for the brief season of the festival. There, about five miles from Mecca, the pilgrims should in imitation of the Prophet spend the night, but it has become customary to continue immediately to 'Arafa, some nine miles further to the east.

'Arafa is a wide plain bounded on the east by a mountain of the same name which, however, is better known as the Mount of Mercy, Jabal ar-Rahma. The mountain rises

150 to 200 feet. Sixty broad stone steps, swerving to the left and then back to the right,[16] lead to a platform. Here on the ninth of the month a dignitary, usually the *qâdî* (judge) of Mecca, mounted on a camel, delivers two *khutbas*. These sermons which are, contrary to the description given by some Western observers, not essential elements of the celebration, fill most of the period of the so-called *wuqûf*—the "standing" (before God)—from the moment when the sun has crossed the meridian to its setting. The *khutbas* consist of what might be called moral platitudes, frequently interrupted by *talbiyas*. They cannot be heard except in the immediate vicinity and at least one European observer (Wavell) never did become aware of their being delivered at all.

The *wuqûf* at 'Arafa, in the terse phrase of tradition, *is* the *hajj;* that is to say, it is its essential ceremony and he who misses it has missed the *hajj*. The plain, deserted the rest of the year, teems with tens and even hundreds of thousands of people. Pious legend puts the number of 'Arafa pilgrims at a constant 700,000—the difference between the actual number of visitors and the ideal is always made up by angels. Tents are pitched, booths set up, and an intense life goes on for a few hours. When sunset approaches the tents are struck and the people wait for "permission," *ijâza*—the signal for the *ifâda*, the "dispersing" to Muzdalifa—about half way back to Minà. "Amid the greatest confusion as the horses are spurred on by the rushing crowd, amid continual shooting and din, accompanied by military music, everyone rushes to Muzdalifa. The *'alamain*, the two pillars or markers, which indicate the boundary of the *haram* are passed; the evening darkness soon falls and torches are kindled; fireworks are discharged and the soldiers keep firing off their guns." [17] Thus tradition has maintained, despite Muhammad's censure of this unrestrained behavior, the pagan pace of the *ifâda*—until the Saudi police suppressed the most dangerous excesses.

In Muzdalifa the night is spent without sleep. The Mosque of Muzdalifa is illuminated. In the morning an-

5. The *Bâb as-Safâ*, facing toward the Hill of Safâ.

From Muhammad Labîb al-Batanûnî, *ar-Riḥla 'l-Hijâziyya*
(2nd ed.), Cairo, 1329/1911.

6. The road between Mecca, Minà, and 'Arafa.

From E. Rutter, *The Holy Cities of Arabia*, London and New York, 1928, G. P. Putnam's Sons.

other *wuqûf* is held, again accompanied by a *khutba*, pronounced by the *qâdî* of Mecca. Meanwhile each pilgrim has collected seventy small pebbles to be used in Minà in the so-called *rajm*, or "Stoning" of the Devils. After he has reached Minà in a second "dispersing," a certain section of which requires the running pace *harwal* obligatory in part of the *sa'y*, he has to throw seven of these at the Jamrat al-'Aqaba, the westernmost and largest of the three *jamarât* (stone-heaps) that are located on the main street of Minà, a couple of hundred yards apart. In pre-Islamic days the *ifâda* to Minà took place at the moment of sunrise, as witness a stray line sung during the course: "Enter into the light of morning, (Mount) Thabîr, so that we may hasten." The Prophet, while accepting the rite in his *hajj*, deprived it of its solar significance by advancing the hour of its performance. The 'Aqaba or, as it is popularly called, the Great Devil, is a crude pillar, three yards high and one yard wide, standing in a basin-like enclosure of more than one yard in height.

This day, the tenth of Dhu 'l-Hijja, is devoted to such ceremonies as are to restore the *muhrim* to the world of the profane. The first of these "desacralizing" rites is the stoning of the 'Aqaba and each throw must be accompanied by the formula: "In the name of Allâh, Allâh is most great." After this stoning the *talbiya* may no longer be used; the *hajj* proper has come to an end, but the pilgrim still has to perform a certain number of rites that are, in the mind of the faithful, inseparable from the *hajj* itself. Above all, he has to sacrifice a sheep, a goat, a bovine or a camel (the last two of which he may share with others). This sacrifice from which the day has received its name, *yaum an-nahr*, may be done anywhere in Minà, but a point near the 'Aqaba is preferred for it was there that Abraham prepared to sacrifice Ishmael (whom Muslim lore substitutes for the Biblical Isaac) when God sent a ram in his stead. So thousands of animals are killed within little more than an hour. It is meritorious to give the flesh to the poor. Actually, a large proportion of the carcasses remains lying around or buried in shallow pits, causing great unpleasantness and an even greater hazard to health, which the government proposes to eliminate by disinfecting the area and by the establishment of an adequate slaughterhouse.[18]

After the sacrifice the pilgrim's head is shaven, but women have their hair cut only slightly. This done, the pilgrim may discard the *ihrâm*. He is now freed from all but sexual restrictions. These are lifted only upon the pilgrim's return to Mecca, the third *ifâda* of the *hajj*, on the same day when he is to perform a *tawâf*. He bathes and has himself sprinkled with Zamzam water before going back to Minà where he is to spend the nights of the eleventh to thirteenth of Dhu 'l-Hijja, the *tashrîq*. *Tashrîq* is a term usually, if unsatisfactorily, explained as "the drying of strips of meat in the sun," to preserve them for use on the homeward journey. These days are devoted to eating, drinking and sensual pleasures. The pilgrim is free to dispose of his time, except that he is obligated to throw each day seven pebbles at each of the three Devils. The stones accumulated during this turbulent procedure are removed to Mecca to serve as gravel in the Great Mosque.[19] The law allows for the shortening of the stay in Minà to two days, but it seems that the present government prefers to keep the pilgrims there for the full period.[20]

Before leaving Mecca for home an *'umrat al-wadâ'*, or farewell *'umra*, is expected of the pilgrim. To consecrate himself he has to take the *ihrâm* at the boundary of the *haram*, usually in at-Tan'îm.

Concurrently with the slaughtering of the animals in Minà and the days of the *tashrîq*, the whole Muslim world celebrates the Great Festival (*al-'îd al-kabîr*) or Sacrificial Feast (*'îd al-adhà* or *'îd al-qurbân*; in Turkish [*büyük*] *bairam*). Every free Muslim who has the means is bidden to sacrifice, but the rite is not a legal duty except in fulfillment of a vow, in which case the sacrificer must not partake of the victim's flesh. Community prayers are held preserving a slightly more archaic form than the ordinary Friday service. New clothes are donned and people bestow presents on one another. The cemeteries are visited and people may even spend the night there camping in tents.

The very tenuous relation between the old ritual and the new religion is striking. Aside perhaps from the ceremonies centering on the Ka'ba, there is no attempt at an ideological or even mythological integration. The practice and precept of the Prophet constitute the only link between Islamic and pre-Islamic worship. Nothing in the doctrine of Islam suggests the *wuqûf* in 'Arafa as the culmination of a specifically Muslim pilgrimage. Pilgrimaging to a sanctuary and "standing" before its Lord is a ritual shared by the Arabs with the Hebrews. "Three times in a year all the males shall appear before the Lord God" (Exodus 23:17). And in the encampment at Sinai the Israelites are required to "sanctify" themselves, wash their clothes and be ready on the third day: "And Moses brought forth the people out of the camp to meet with God; and they stood at the nether part of the mount" (Exodus 19:17). Muhammad altered the pagan character of the 'Arafa *wuqûf* by declaring the whole of the plain a *mauqif*, "a place of standing" before God, rather than the limited area sacred to the original deity of the locality. Similarly he adapted the sacrifice at Minà to his own uses by taking it away from the local deity and declaring the whole of Minà *manhar*—a place of sacrifice.

Although nothing is known about the divinity which Islam displaced at 'Arafa, it appears highly probable that it was the sun-demon who was driven out by the ceremony of stoning. The fight against the scorching sun at Minà connects well with the rite in honor of the fertilizing thunder-god Quzah at Muzdalifa. The designation of the eighth of Dhu 'l-Hijja as *yaum at-tarwiya*, the Day of Moistening—now somewhat flatly explained as the day on which the pilgrims provide themselves with water for the festival—would suggest a rain-making ceremony, a last vestige of which might be discovered in the sprinkling of the pilgrim with zamzam water.

It would hardly have been possible for the new religion

to adopt these rites, had their original meaning not already been dimmed in the worshipers' minds. The same can be said of the *'umra*, literally "cult," which incidentally in Islam has always maintained a position apart. Not a "pillar" of the faith, the *'umra* has retained something of a voluntary character, of an act of personal devotion above and beyond duty. But it has, from the pagan point of view, lost its original point by its combination with the *sa'y*, as well as by the abolition of the sacrifice at the Ka'ba which at one time formed an indispensable part of it. For, in its origin, the *'umra* was a festival of firstlings. Like Passover, it was held in early spring, in the month Rajab, which Islam endeavored to replace by its own sacred month, Ramadân. As late as the twelfth century, however, the local population preferred performance of the *'umra* in Rajab to any other time, though the connection between the nature of the festival and its timing had long since been forgotten. Similarly, although the basic features of the *hajj* ritual are in a sense divorced from the basic dogma of Islam, this in no way lessens the extremely effective hold the Pilgrimage had, and has, over the minds and hearts of the faithful.

It is perhaps not commonly realized how much hardship is involved in making the Pilgrimage to Mecca in the traditional style. The discomfort and strain of caravan travel through an inhospitable countryside in a difficult climate is increased by the religious exaltation, in the last stages by the wearing of the *ihrâm* and, above all, by the constant threat of Bedouin attacks. It was not until some twenty years ago when the Saudi power was established throughout northern and western Arabia, that the pilgrims could be sure of their safety. Before that, the various governments, or the leaders of the individual caravans, had been compelled to buy off the Bedouins by paying them for protecting the caravan on its way through their customary pasture grounds, and even such arrangements in no wise guaranteed the travelers an unmolested journey. In our day the use of steamers, busses and even airplanes, reduces the length of the *hajj* comfortably and the kind of pilgrimage-travel of which it was said that it was "a sort of punishment" is gradually falling into disuse.

The Syrian caravan usually took about thirty days, and the Egyptian, thirty-seven. Such a caravan, often made up of some six thousand travelers of all walks of life, would journey under an *amîr al-hajj*, "commander of the Pilgrimage," who was appointed by his government. He not only directed the journey, but supervised the conduct of the pilgrims and led his contingent of *hâjji's* during the ceremonies. He also inherited from such pilgrims as might die en route whatever goods they had brought along. The official who brought their annual payment to the numerous Meccan pensioners on the dotation rolls of Constantinople and Cairo served on his staff.

The departure as well as the return of the caravan is usually marked by very elaborate celebrations. In Egypt, for example, some three weeks before the caravan was to leave, the *kiswa* (the curtain of the Ka'ba) was paraded in a preliminary festivity. A few days before the caravan actually set out, there was another procession centering about the *mahmal* (or more strictly, *mahmil*), which can perhaps be briefly characterized as a richly adorned ceremonial litter which is to accompany the caravan to the Holy Places and back. E. W. Lane's famous description of 1835 still holds good:

"It is a square skeleton-frame of wood, with a pyramidal top; and has a covering of black brocade, richly worked with inscriptions and ornamental embroidery in gold, in some parts upon a ground of green and red silk, and bordered with a fringe of silk, with tassels surmounted by silver bells. Its covering is not always made after the same pattern with regard to the decorations; but in every cover that I have seen, I have remarked, on the upper part of the front, a view of the Temple of Mekkeh, worked in gold; and, over it, the Sultan's cypher. It contains nothing; but has two *mushafs* (or copies of the Koran), one on a scroll, and the other in the usual form of a little book, and each enclosed in a case of gilt silver, attached, externally, at the top. . . . The Mahmal is borne by a fine tall camel, which is generally indulged with exemption from every kind of labor during the remainder of its life."

The *mahmal* used to be followed by the Shaikh of the Camel, an almost naked man mounted on a camel, who was believed to roll his head throughout the journey. Up to a few years before Lane's visit, "there used also to follow the Mahmal, to and from Mekkeh, an old woman, with her head uncovered, and only wearing a shirt. She was called the Mother of the Cats, having always five or six cats sitting about her on her camel." [21] The Mother of the Cats was later replaced by a Father of the Cats. It would be difficult to interpret this usage otherwise than as a survival from the ancient Egyptian pilgrimage to Bubastis in the Delta, mentioned by Herodotus, during which it was customary to bring cats to the goddess whom the Greek historian identified with Artemis.[22]

The *mahmal*, which at the beginning of this century cost the Egyptian government in the neighborhood of $250,000, is the object of great reverence and, especially at its return, people seek to touch it in order to partake of its virtue, *baraka*. The origin of the *mahmal* is not certain, but it is likely to represent a development of the portable sanctuaries of the pagan Arabs which, incidentally, have in some regions survived to this day and constitute in wanderings and in war the visible center of the tribe. The Egyptian *mahmal* is attested to since the thirteenth century. In this period it became a symbol of sovereignty and independence and not only the Egyptian but the Syrian, Iraqi and Yemeni caravans brought *mahmals* to Mecca and 'Arafa.

The special prestige enjoyed by the Egyptian *mahmal* reflects the political preponderance of Egypt in the Hijâz during the 250 years since the custom was first recorded. The Syrian *mahmal* was discontinued after the First World War. The Saudi government protested the armed guard of the Egyptian *mahmal* as an infringement of its sovereignty and for a number of years Egypt suspended the sending of both *maḥmal* and *kiswa*. But the old custom has since been restored.

The Egyptian polyhistor, as-Suyûtî (d. 1505), quotes the Secretary of State, Ibn Fadl Allâh (d. 1348) to the effect that the caravan would set out from Cairo with food and water supplies, with medicines and drugs, physicians and oculists, and washers of the dead.[23] The health problem inherent in the Pilgrimage has been plaguing the governments concerned, especially since the first outbreaks of the cholera in Europe in 1830 and 1837 which were traceable to infection carried back from Mecca by the returning pilgrims. Quarantine stations were organized at both ends of the Red Sea and various controls instituted, but the success of the measures was at best a moderate one. This was due in part to the lukewarm cooperation of the Ottoman government, then in control of the Holy Places, and was aggravated by the fact that European personnel was not admitted to the sites of the Pilgrimage, but in part also to the impossibility of policing all the land routes to Mecca. In addition to those European governments that held colonies with large Muslim populations, it was Egypt particularly that worked for the improvement of sanitary conditions in the Hijâz in order to protect its own citizens from contagion.

These endeavors have led to occasional tensions with the Saudi government which resented the foreign interference and the criticism it implied. But Ibn Saud has done more than any of his predecessors to make the Pilgrimage safe from the medical point of view. A bacteriological station has been opened in Jidda. The hospitals in the major towns were reorganized, ambulances set up, and the quarantine service improved throughout the country. In addition, rest stations with wells and dispensaries have been placed at the pilgrims' disposal as well as hotels in places like Mecca and Minà. Much remains to be done, but the progress achieved is considerable.

The Saudi government has also created a school for guides. These guides (*mutawwif*, literally: the person who conducts the *tawâf*) are indispensable to the foreign visitors of whom they take complete charge, often from their landing in Jidda until their departure for home. The *mutawwif* provides accommodations for the pilgrim and the mount he may need to reach the outlying points such as 'Arafa and at-Tan'îm. He sees to it that the complicated rites are correctly performed, with the accompaniment of the prescribed or customary invocations. Since the majority of the pilgrims are not Arabs this is not always an easy task. The *mutawwif's* are organized as a guild headed by a shaikh to whom suitable presents have to be made. They are taxed by the government. The guild is divided into groups, each assigned to pilgrims of a certain nationality or region—and thus each guide is perfectly familiar with the habits of his clients who always hail from the same rather limited region. The number of foreign pilgrims has hardly ever fallen below 50,000 to 60,000; and it is on the services required by them that Mecca subsists. But a lean year for Mecca is also a lean year for Saudi Arabia, although by now the oil royalties have notably diminished the importance of the income derived from the *hajj*.

Owing to its religious and cultural function, the Mother of Cities, as the Koran calls Mecca, plays an important part in the crystallization and transmission of Muslim opinion, less perhaps in issues of practical politics than in the formation of those attitudes which in the long run will determine the direction of movements of thought. As a theological center it is unquestionably conservative.

When Ibn Saud took over Mecca in 1924, the Muslim world followed the events with a certain tenseness—in 1925 only 3,000 pilgrims came by sea from abroad. For the Saudi Arabians are Wahhâbis, that is puritan sectarians inimical to any deviation from Koranic precept. Consequently, they are actively hostile, not only to the luxuries of life, but to the traditional veneration of personages of the "heroic age" of Islam—the "sanctification" of the Prophet, and a great many customs connected with the *hajj* for which the Book does not provide sufficient evidence. The Wahhâbis had occupied Mecca twice in the early years of the nineteenth century and the radicalism with which they had suppressed what they considered superstitious practice had not been forgotten. But Ibn Saud left the Pilgrimage intact and the regained confidence of the Muslim world expressed itself almost at once in the number of foreign visitors to the Holy Places. In spite of the deliberate efforts of the Saudi government to attract pilgrims, the economic crisis of the thirties, the Second World War, and possibly a weakening of the devotional impulse in some of the Muslim countries, have made participation in the *hajj* during the second quarter of our century considerably smaller than during the first quarter.

Upon completion of the *hajj*, the pilgrim is advised not to linger in Mecca but to return home without delay. There are those who remain in the Mother of Cities for years to live and study as "neighbors of God," but most faithful are likely to grow careless in reverence by prolonged and easy familiarity with the Sanctuary and the inevitable insight into the less commendable aspects of Meccan life. And then, while good deeds done in Mecca count for more than good deeds done elsewhere, this increased efficacy of man's actions applies to sins as well, so a protracted stay may not be without its hazards. On his return the pilgrim, who will add the epithet *hâjj* to his name, will be met with joy and respect, possibly in a festive and ceremonial manner. In general, his prestige in the community will be increased and, in the outlying regions of the Muslim world, he will become a center of religious fervor and missionary activity.

What actually is the nature of the pilgrim's religious experience? What spiritual content does he find in that intricate system of rites? The consciousness of fulfilling a fundamental obligation and of taking a significant step toward the attainment of eternal bliss is there, of course; but the emotional response is bound to be more differentiated in its association with the individual phases of the *hajj*. During the culminating collective ceremonies, the pilgrims are gripped by an intense feeling of unity, of the strength and grandeur of their faith, and by the majesty of the Lord to which they respond with passionate submission.

"The whole assembly stood there [in prayer at the Ka'ba] in the greatest reverence before this highest majesty and most powerful inspirer of awe before which the greatest souls become so little as to be almost nothing. And if we had not been witness of the movements of the body during the *salât* and the raising of the hands during the prayers, and the murmurings of the expressions of humility and if we had not heard the beating of the hearts before this immeasurable grandeur we would have thought ourselves transferred to another life. And truly we were at that hour in another world: we were in the house of God and in God's immediate presence, and with us were only the lowered head and the humble tongue and the voices raised in prayer and weeping eyes and the fearful heart and pure thoughts of intercession [by the Prophet]." God is everywhere, yet: "the Ka'ba is His temple and the place of His grandeur and grace. And is there in any of the four quarters of the earth a place not quite seven square miles in extent where half a million people assemble on a pilgrimage, all of whom call to God with one heart and one tongue? And although they differ in race and language, they all turn toward one *qibla* and at the *salât* move with one motion, without any hope other than the grace of the one God, who has not begotten and is not born and is without equal" [cf. Koran 112].[24]

Paganism has been banned from the Holy Places for more than thirteen hundred years. But the peculiar mood of pagan piety still colors the emotion of the Bedouin worshipers. The Koran is full of distrust of the religious potential of the nomad. *The Bedouins say: "We have believed." Say: "Ye have not believed, but say ye rather, 'We have become Muslims;' for belief has not yet entered your hearts"* (Koran 49:14). Muhammad's estimate of their religious educability is borne out by the report of the traveler, Ibn Jubair, who witnessed the following scene during his own Pilgrimage in 1182.

Ten days before the Festival, several thousand Yemenite tribesmen arrive in Mecca to combine bartering of victuals with an *'umra*. They believe that the fertility of their country is due to the *baraka* they bring back from their visit to the Holy House—"so they are on this account in a profitable trade relation with Allâh. Their purposes are not directed by the traditional precepts of the Law, nor would you find with them any of the (legal) devotional practices except for the sincerity of their intention. When they make the *tawâf* around the sacred Ka'ba they throw themselves on it as children do on a gentle mother—they seek shelter in closeness to it, attach themselves to its curtains and where their hands cling they tear because of the vehemence of their pull . . ." All the while, however, they offer prayers of such fervor that the bystanders'break into tears. But as long as they are in town no one besides them is able to perform the *tawâf* or to touch the Black Stone. Thirty or forty of them hold on to one another as tightly as if they were connected by chains. And when in mounting to the door of the Ka'ba this "chain" breaks at one point they all tumble down—a laughable sight. Their prayer is the most amusing of all the funny things Bedouins will do. They will face the Ka'ba and prostrate themselves once or twice or even four times hitting the ground hard with their foreheads and completely disregarding the prescribed order of movements. Then they will lift their heads a little above the ground turning left and right as if in fright. Then they will get up without having pronounced the *shahâda* and sometimes even without having said the "desacralizing" greeting of the believers, the *salâm*, which is the final phase of the correct *salât*. While they are praying they will call out to one another and exchange observations in a loud voice.[25]

In 1909, Batanûnî observed that the Bedouins from the East appeared to feel that the pilgrimage was accomplished at the Ka'ba rather than at 'Arafa. They, too, perform the *tawâf* in bands holding each other by the hand. They disregard whoever else might be on the *matâf* shouting while they proceed: Allâh! Muhammad! At Thy service! At Thy service! I perform the *hajj*—you accept it or not! I perform the *hajj*—will you accept it? The women are clutched to the backs of the men. When they reach the Black Stone they all touch and kiss it. The husband knocks the head of his wife against the stone so that she will bear a visible mark of having made her *hajj*. At the same time he cries out to her: "Have you made the *hajj*, Oh *hâjja* [female pilgrim]?" She replies: "I have, I have!" Then she turns to the Black Stone, saying: "I have made the *hajj*—tell your Master that I have made the *hajj*." Lifting her head toward the sky, she continues: "Whether you accept me or not, I have made the *hajj*. If you do not accept of me—you will have to accept!" [26]

It remained for Ghazzâlî to interpret the spiritual meaning of the Pilgrimage as a whole and in its individual phases.

The first requirement, for the pilgrim, is to understand what the *hajj* means within religion as a whole. There is no access to God except through self-abnegation. For this reason the religious of earlier faiths withdrew from the world. When this tendency weakened, Muhammad was sent to revive the tradition; but, as the Prophet explained, in exchange for monasticism the Lord gave the Muslims Holy War and the Pilgrimage. He honored the House in Mecca by connecting it with Himself and appointed it the goal of visitors from all regions who were to come in a spirit of humility before His majesty, while acknowledging that no House or country could confine Him.

In order that they might make their journey a more eloquent testimonial to their devotion, He imposed on them actions which were not in themselves appealing intellectually or emotionally, like the stoning of the "Devils" and the *sa'y*. The poor-tax is a precept that is intellectually acceptable, fasting is an effective means of fighting desire, the tool of the devil, and *salât* is a natural gesture of submission and glorification. However, the

merit of executing commands that appeal neither to the
feelings nor to reason lies in its effectiveness in the purification of the heart. To wonder at the strange doings prescribed is to be unaware of the true mysteries of devotional practice.

The pilgrim who sets out for the Ka'ba should bear in
mind that he goes to see the Lord and that, by the Lord's
own promise, the sight of the House will be accepted as
a claim to being vouchsafed the sight of the Lord's face
in the world to come. The longing to be in the sight of
God in the next world incites the longing to bring this
meeting about by making the Pilgrimage in this world,
even though the lover will seek the presence of the beloved without looking toward a reward. So the pilgrim
must impress upon himself the magnitude of his under-
taking and make sure of his single-mindedness in his task
and the purity of his motivation. He is to cut his ties with
his own small world and, in doing so, he must make good
the wrongs he has done with sincere repentance. Would
you want to go to the palace of the king, if you have neg-
lected his command in your home? Would you not be
ashamed to approach him as a rebellious slave and be
driven away? Uproot your attachment to your home and
homeland. Go as if you were never to return! Do not take
too many provisions! Rather bethink yourself of that
other journey into the next world, for which your only
provision is fear of God. Treat your mount well and
always think of that other journey, your funeral, when
you will be carried on it—perhaps even before completing
your Pilgrimage.

You may meet God before you reach the House. Even
as the believer will some day meet God in a garment he
does not wear in this life, that is, the shroud, so the pilgrim goes to the House in an unusual garment—the *ihrâm*.
Both are alike in that they are unsewn. On the journey
the pilgrim should hope for acceptance, not in virtue of
his own acts, but trusting in God's grace and the fulfillment of His promise. The *talbiya* is the answer to God's
summons and should remind the faithful of the response

of the people to the trumpet on the Day of Resurrection, when they will rise from their graves and assemble in uncertainty about their ultimate fate. Upon entering the Holy Territory, the pilgrim should both hope for safety from punishment and fear that he might be considered unworthy of the Lord's proximity—but hope should be stronger than fear. In the House, he should endeavor to apprehend the Lord of the House and give thanks to Him for allowing him to reach that far.

"And call to mind . . . the pouring forth of people on the Day of Resurrection toward Paradise all hoping to enter it, and how then they will be divided in those that are admitted and those that are turned away [paralleling the event] with the dividing of the pilgrims in those whose pilgrimage will be accepted and those whose pilgrimage will be refused. Never neglect for a moment to be reminded of the other world by anything you see: for all the states of the *hajj* point to the states of the other world."

The *tawâf* is *salât*. Realize that by the *tawâf* you come to resemble the angels that are circling the Throne. The purpose is not the *tawâf* of your body around the House, but the *tawâf* of your heart around the Lord of the House. Thus the *tawâf* sanctifies the pilgrim. In touching the Black Stone, you are doing homage to God, as it has been said: "The Black Stone is God's right hand on earth." The repeated course between Safâ and Marwa resembles the repeated efforts of the servant at the court of the king to show his sincerity in service and his hope to be looked upon with the eye of mercy. In his uncertainty, he retraces his steps coming and going. Let him think in shuttling between the two hills of himself hanging in balance on the Day of Judgment, let Safâ symbolize for him his good works and Marwa the bad, and let him move as between punishment and forgiveness.

In 'Arafa, the crowds, the shouting, the many tongues, the grouping of the nations by their leaders should remind you of the plains of the Last Day when the nations will assemble around their prophets, desirous of their intercession, fearful and perplexed. Be humble, but hopeful. When all unite their yearnings, do not think God will disappoint them. It has been said that to "stand" in 'Arafa and not to believe that God has forgiven you is a very great sin. When you throw the pebbles, be motivated by obedience only; try to be as Abraham was, when the Devil appeared to him to inject doubt in his heart and induce him to rebel, and Abraham stoned the Devil at God's behest. Should you think that Abraham was faced by Satan, and you are not—know that this very thought is given you by Satan who wants you to think the pelting to be a meaningless play. Outwardly you are casting pebbles at the 'Aqaba, but in reality you are smiting Satan by your increased obedience to God's command. Realize, finally, that sacrifice will draw you near to Him in virtue of your obedience. Be hopeful that, for each limb of the victim, God will free one of your limbs from the Fire.

When the *hajj* is duly completed, fear must lodge in the pilgrim's heart, for he does not know whether his *hajj* has been accepted or not. But he will obtain certainty from his heart and his own actions. For, if he finds himself moving away from delusion and doing right in the light of the Law, he may be sure of acceptance. For God accepts only those whom He loves, and whom He loves He befriends openly and manifests in him the effects of His love, keeping him the while from Satan's assaults. May God protect us from having our pilgrimage rejected!

Modern theologians do not seem to have reached beyond Ghazzâlî's conception.[27]

It is the mystics who go one step further in the interpretation of the *hajj*. Hujwîrî (d. *ca.* 1072) explains: "The sacred territory is so called because it contains the Station of Abraham [the Maqâm Ibrâhîm]. Abraham had two stations: the station of the body, namely, Mecca, and the station of his soul, namely, friendship [with God]." Whoever seeks his bodily station must go through the ceremonies of the Pilgrimage. "But whoever seeks his spiritual station must renounce familiar associations and bid farewell to pleasures and take no thought of other than of God; then he must stand on the 'Arafât of gnosis and from there set out for the Muzdalifa of amity and from there send out his heart to circumambulate the temple of Divine purification and throw away the stones of passion and corrupt thoughts in the Minà of faith, and sacrifice his lower self on the altar of mortification and arrive at the station of friendship." [28]

But others were not satisfied with this kind of moralistic allegory. Muhammad b. al-Fadl of Balkh said: "I wonder at those who seek His Temple in this world: why do not they seek contemplation of Him in their hearts? The temple they sometimes attain and sometimes miss, but contemplation they might enjoy always. If they are bound to visit a stone, which is looked at only once a year, surely they are more bound to visit the temple of the heart, where He may be seen three hundred and sixty times in a day and night." [29]

When al-Hallâj was accused of heresy (and finally executed in 922), one of the impugned tenets was his alleged abrogation of the duty to accomplish the Pilgrimage to Mecca, since God was everywhere and the intention of the lawgiver was but to make man turn to Him. He was charged with having expressed himself to the effect that a person who meant to perform the *hajj* could take the *ihrâm* in his house, recite certain formulae and prayers, read sections of the Koran, execute some *tawâf's*, and so forth, with the result that this rite would absolve him from the obligation of actually visiting the Holy Places. At his trial Hallâj declared that he had only repeated an older tradition; besides, the ceremony described was meant only for those whom poverty prevented from making the actual Pilgrimage.[30]

Whatever Hallâj's intention may have been, it appears as the almost inevitable outgrowth of that mystical attitude which, some centuries later, was poignantly articulated by Ibn al-'Arabî (d. 1240) when he observed that the true Ka'ba was nothing but our own being.

The Law could never dispense with the tenet that the

7. The Mount of Mercy in 'Arafa.

From Muhammad Labîb al-Batanûnî, *ar-Riḥla 'l-Hijâziyya* (2nd ed.), Cairo, 1329/1911.

8. Minà.

From Batanûnî.

9. The stoning of the Second Devil in Minà.
From Batanûnî.

10. The *Masjid al-Khaif* in Minà.
From Batanûnî.

precept must be literally executed and the action literally understood. Yet already in the ninth century Bâyazîd Bistâmî (d. 874) had thus described the progress of the true pilgrim: "On my first pilgrimage I saw only the temple; the second time, I saw both the temple and the Lord of the temple; and the third time I saw the Lord alone." [31]

iii . Ramadân

WHILE THE OBLIGATION TO MAKE THE PIL-
grimage can be actually fulfilled only by a part of the
faithful, the obligation of fasting through the month of
Ramadân—the fourth of the so-called "Pillars of the
Faith"—profoundly affects the life of every believer. In
fact, this *saum*, or Fasting, has come to be regarded by
many as the most important religious act and is kept by
many Muslims who are inclined to neglect even their
daily prayers.

The same Judaeo-Christian influences, which had even
before Muhammad induced individual God-seekers to
lead an ascetic mode of life, are likely to have suggested
to the Muslim community the early adoption of fasting
as a means of spiritual discipline. But it was only after
Muhammad had in Medina obtained closer acquaintance
with the details of Jewish practice that he ordered his
followers to fast on *'Ashûrâ*—the Day of Atonement
(tenth of Tishri). Later, the Day of Atonement became
identified with the Tenth of Muharram—the first month of
the Muslim year. Soon afterward his relations with the
Jewish tribes deteriorated and in the second year of the
hijra a revelation abolished the *'Ashûrâ* fast, replacing it
by the obligation to fast "a certain number of days" during the month of Ramadân (Koran 2:180).

For the next four or five years the Muslims still followed the Jewish custom of fasting from sunset to sunset. But then a new revelation modified the practice by
prescribing: . . . *eat and drink until so much of the dawn*

51

*appears that a white thread may be distinguished from a
black; then keep the fast completely until night* (Koran
2:183). This lightening of the believer's burden extends
to sexual relations, abstention from which had from the
beginning been included in the concept of *saum*. The
redefinition of the limits of fasting within each twenty-
four-hour period seems to have been accompanied by its
prolongation from an indefinite number of days (pre-
sumably ten, in analogy to the ten days of fasting and
prayer that precede the Day of Atonement) to the full
twenty-nine days of Ramadân. The Tenth of Muharram,
however, retained its special character to some extent in
that voluntary fasting on that day was recommended as
especially meritorious.

The Ramadân Fast has been likened to the Christian
Quadragesima and also to Manichaean practices, but it
should be remembered that the "holy" month was a
familiar concept in pagan Arabia, although no rite is
known to have continued through the whole of any of
the pre-Islamic holy months. Ramadân was selected because it was in this month, the fifth of the Muslim year,
that *the Koran was sent down as guidance for the people*
(Koran 2:181). More accurately, the first revelation occurred in the *lailat al-qadr*, or Night of Power, commonly
identified with that of the twenty-seventh of Ramadân.
The Koran describes this night as *better than a thousand
months*. The angels and spirits descend to earth and *it is
peace until the rising of the dawn* (Koran 97:3, 5).

Ramadân, the "Scorcher," had been held especially
sacred in pre-Islamic days. As its name indicates, it fell
in summer. The period preceding and following the
summer-solstice appears to have been distinguished by
religious observances. Its center was the Fifteenth of
Sha'bân, the eighth month, which to our day "has preserved some features of a New Year's day." [1] The chronological as well as the functional relation between that
day and the beginning of Ramadân strongly resembles
that of New Year and the Day of Atonement in the

Jewish calendar. To understand the full significance of the parallelism, it must be kept in mind that the year of the pagan Arabs was lunisolar: Its lunar months kept their place in relation to the seasons by the addition, every second or third year, of a thirteenth month. Defective astronomical knowledge interfered, however, with the actual operation of time-reckoning—in Muhammad's day the time of the *hajj* that had originally been associated with autumn had moved forward into spring.

Shortly before his death the Prophet, prompted by a revelation, constituted the Muslim year to be a sequence of twelve lunar months, totaling 354 days, so that thirty-three Muslim years equal approximately thirty-two of our solar years. Consequently, each Muslim month moves through the seasons in about thirty-three years. This rotation not only adds periodically to the hardship of *saum* and *hajj* by placing them at the height of the summer heat, but also removes the Muslim festivals completely from whatever connection with natural phenomena their pagan origins may have had. The Jewish calendar, on the other hand, keeps the New Year within the autumn season.

On the religious level Ramadân parallels Yôm Kippur in that it constitutes a period of atonement and forgiveness. Tradition has it that during Ramadân the gates of Heaven are opened, the gates of Hell closed, and the devils put in chains. And it expresses the belief that whosoever observes the Ramadân Fast faithfully and with pure intention will obtain remission of his sins. It is not only fasting as such that is meritorious and effective in cleansing the believer's heart, but fasting in Ramadân is said to be thirty times better than at any other period.

In Jewish legend the world was created on New Year's day. No cosmological significance attaches to the First of Muharram, the official opening of the Muslim year. But the night of the Fifteenth of Sha'bân, *lailat al-barâ'a* (behind which hitherto unexplained term the Hebrew *berî'a*, "creation," may be concealed [2]) has preserved associations characteristic of a New Year's festival. In India and Indonesia the day is set aside for the dead. In

Egypt it is believed that the Lotus-Tree at the Boundary, which stands at the extremity of Paradise and has as many leaves as there are human beings in the world, each leaf inscribed with the name of one person, "is shaken on this night, a little after sunset; and when a person is destined to die in the ensuing year, his leaf . . . falls on this occasion." A special prayer is said by the Muslim immediately after the evening-prayer on that night. A chapter of the Koran (Sûra 36) is recited and an invocation intoned which "culminates in this supplication: O God, if Thou have recorded me in Thy abode miserable, or unfortunate, or scanted in my sustenance, cancel, O God, of Thy goodness, my misery, and misfortune and scanty allowance of sustenance, and confirm me in Thy abode . . . as happy, and provided for, and directed to good." [3]

In Persia, and under Persian influence in Iraq, Syria and even Egypt, New Year was for some time celebrated in spring. The learned frowned, but the people would not be deterred. At the Court in Baghdad, the caliph distributed roses made of red amber. Mutawakkil (847-861) reputedly struck five million dirhems (small silver coins) painted in various colors, red, yellow, black, for showering upon his officials.[4] Masked actors appeared before the ruler who flung coins at them. In Persia, al-Bêrûnî (wrote *ca.* 1008) informs us, "People rose on this day early, at the rising of the dawn, and went to the water of the aqueducts and wells. Frequently, too, they drew running water in a vase, and poured it over themselves, considering this a good omen and a means to keep off hurt. On the same day people sprinkle water over each other, of which the cause is said to be the same as that of the washing." According to another report, Bêrûnî continues, the reason for it was that once after a long drought, rain fell on New Year's Day—"Therefore they considered the rain a good omen, and poured it over each other, which has remained among them as a custom. According to another explanation, this water-sprinkling simply holds the place of a purification, by which people cleansed their bodies from the smoke of fire and from the dirt connected with attending to the fires [in winter]. Besides it serves the purpose of removing from the air that corruption which produces epidemic and other diseases." [5]

In fifteenth-century Egypt the people used to assemble before the royal palace on New Year's Day. With their musical instruments they made a gruesome noise and, disregarding the Koranic interdiction, they drank publicly wine and other intoxicants.[6] In Cairo, the Persian *naurûz* (New Year) customs were combined with practices typical of a Saturnalia or a Carnival festival. The people nominated a "Prince of the New Year" who "besmeared his face with flour or lime, went through the streets on a donkey, in a red or yellow coat, with a copy-book in hand like a market-inspector collecting money from the well-to-do. He who did not pay had water or dirt thrown at him. They hit each other with straps and twisted leather-ropes, the poor in the streets, the rich in their houses. The police, therefore, entertained no complaints on that score. In the school the teacher was attacked by the students and sometimes thrown into a fountain where he remained until he redeemed himself by payment." [7] It was only late in the fourteenth century that the government succeeded in suppressing the Carnival features of the festival. The Copts have, however, retained *naurûz* as their New Year's Day, but its actual date has fallen in line with the indigenous tradition and is placed on the tenth or eleventh of September.

These contradictory computations of the New Year are an instructive illustration of the sometimes rather casual coexistence of Islamic habits of thought and traditional pre-Islamic patterns of behavior. The best the theologians could do was to suggest a tie connecting the pagan survival with an incident of Muslim history or legend. Thus the sprinkling at *naurûz* was accounted for as a commemoration of the swallows sprinkling water for joy, when Solomon recovered his signet-ring that had been stolen from him by an evil demon. On this analogy, it seems likely that the *lailat al-qadr* fell in Ramadân because of the age-old sanctity of the month, and not because the Revelation, commencing on that particular night, made the whole month sacred, as the Muslim tradition would have us believe.

The importance attributed to fasting is reflected in Ghazzâlî's saying that it represents one-fourth of faith, for the Prophet said: Fasting is one half of endurance, and he also said: endurance is one half of faith.[8] And the Prophet is also credited with the observation that the foul smell of the faster's mouth is sweeter before God than the scent of musk. But fasting as such is not enough. Abstention must be practiced in conformance with the precepts of the legalists. The majority of the canon authorities require renewal of the *niyya* before dawn on each day of Ramadân. The *muftirât*, a term covering the total body of incidents breaking or invalidating the Fast, include above all "the entering into the body of any material substances in so far as it is done consciously and is preventable." [9] Thus, the swallowing of food and drink, the inhaling of tobacco and even the swallowing of one's spittle (if it is possible to eject it) are prohibited. The prohibition applies, too, to injections of any kind into the body. Somewhat strangely, deliberate vomiting is also forbidden. Even if it is done on doctor's orders, the day is considered lost and has to be made good later. The other principal *muftirât* are sexual relations, intoxication and menstruation.

The obligation to fast begins on the First of Ramadân, which follows after the twenty-ninth or the thirtieth of Sha'bân, depending on when evidence of one trustworthy witness that he has seen the new moon is brought to the *qâdî*. The beginning of the Ramadân has to be announced to the people, according to local custom, by gunshot, the hanging of lamps in the minarets and the like. Except for young children, only the aged and the sick, nursing or pregnant women, and travelers on a prolonged journey are exempt from fasting. But the law is extremely strict in demanding that missed days be made good upon recovery after weaning, or on returning.

It is recommended that the faster break his fast as soon as he is certain that the sun has set, for continuous fasting is forbidden. He also should avoid actions which, while not actually forbidden, might arouse passion in oneself or in others. Although he may hold water in his mouth for a moment, he should refrain from tasting or chewing anything edible as well as from being cupped or bled. If possible, he should practice *i'tikâf*, that is, withdraw to a mosque, especially during the last ten days of the month during which, probably on an odd day and most likely on the Twenty-seventh, the *lailat al-qadr* occurred. Prayer and recitation of the Koran are to fill this period of retreat.

Ghazzâlî explains the special meritoriousness of fasting by the fact that, unlike all other devotional acts, it is visible only to God. Furthermore, it is a potent means of defeating Satan. For the passions that are Satan's weapons are strengthened by eating and drinking. To beat down God's enemy is to assist God. And *if ye help Allah He will help you, and set firm your feet* (Koran 47:8). The Prophet of God has said: Were it not for the devils flying about the hearts of men, they would readily look to the kingdom of heaven. Thus, fasting becomes the "gateway of divine service."

Speaking of "the mysteries of the fast," Ghazzâlî makes it clear that punctilious observance of the external law does not exhaust the real intention of the lawgiver. Actually, fasting has three degrees: First, that of the common crowd which does not go beyond literal execution of the stipulations of the law. The second consists in keeping all one's senses and members from sin. The third implies abstention from all aspirations regarding this world and withdrawal of the heart from anything except the Lord. On this level the fast is broken by thinking of anything but God, the Last Day, and the world in relation to them. This is the station of the prophets and saints—it represents the realization throughout life of the Koranic injunction: *Say: "Allah," and leave them* [i.e., mankind] *in their discussion playing about* (Koran 6:91).

The second degree, however, suffices for the pious. It demands that the believer avoid thinking of anything reprehensible and of anything that might distract him from the remembrance of God. Five things, the Prophet said, annul the Fast: A lie, backbiting, slander, a false oath, and a glance of passion. Indecent and dishonest talk or action, hostile and hypocritical behavior must be avoided—concentration on the name of God and the recitation of the Book is the fast of the tongue. Nor may you listen to discussion of evil: what must not be said must not be listened to. When the physical fast is broken, the normal measure of food should not be exceeded. Overeating at night will but strengthen the passions fasting is designed to curb. The contemplation of the Kingdom of Heaven is not possible when there is a barrier of food between chest and heart, nor does an empty table suffice to lift that barrier as long as the faster's aspiration swerves from God. Like the pilgrim, the faster should remain in suspense between fear and hope, since he does not know if his fast will be accepted. Man's position is between animal and angel. Each time he succumbs to passion his position is lowered, each time he overcomes it, he rises toward the angels. Therefore it has been said: "How many fasters there are for whom only hunger and thirst are the results of their fast!"

Both the legalists and Ghazzâlî are explicit in their statements as to which days are most propitious for a voluntary fast. Dhu 'l-Hijja, Muharram, Rajab and Sha'bân—all deriving their sanctity ultimately from pre-Islamic lore—are the preferred months. In each month, the first, the last, the twelfth, and the days of the white nights (the thirteenth through the fifteenth) are the favorite days. In each week, Monday, Thursday and Friday are especially appropriate. It is perhaps worth noting that, in including Friday, Ghazzâlî runs counter to the law, which expresses the fear that fasting on Friday will distract people from the community service. In general, fasting on festive days is recommended; but it is forbidden during the days of

tashrîq in Minà and on the days of the Great and the Little
Festivals.

"Life-long" fasting, as it was practiced by some of the
mystics in Ghazzâlî's time, is not looked upon with favor;
for the sequence of the fast should be broken on occasion,
such as during the *tashrîq*, or even regularly. But, if it is
felt that one's spiritual welfare hinges on continual fasting, no objection should be raised. Nevertheless, fasting
on alternate days or at three-day intervals is more highly
recommended. In fact, Ghazzâlî considers it much more
difficult a form of asceticism. To the elect, fasting is but
a means. "The fruit of hunger is contemplation of God,
of which the forerunner is mortification. Repletion combined with contemplation is better than hunger combined
with mortification, because contemplation is the battlefield of men, whereas mortification is the playground of
children." [10]

The actual performance of the Ramadân Fast varies, of
course, to a certain extent from country to country. A
fairly adequate idea of what this "fourth pillar" of Islam
involves in terms of the daily lives of the observing faithful can be gained from the colorful narratives of such
travelers as E. W. Lane (who lived in Cairo from 1825–28
and again from 1833–35); Sir Richard Burton (Cairo,
1853); C. Snouck Hurgronje and Eldon Rutter, who
stayed in Mecca in 1884–85, and 1925–26, respectively.

It was on the fifteenth of March, 1926, that Ramadân
was proclaimed to Rutter and his fellow Muslims. Already
the summer heat was hovering over the city of Mecca. At
once life took on a different aspect. "Every night at about
the hour of half-past eight by Arabic time [the Arabic day
begins at 6 P.M.—2:30 A.M. our time], in the darkness before dawn, a gun was fired from the Fort of Jiyâd. This
gave notice of the arrival of the hour of the *sahûr*, the
meal before dawn. Two hours later, the gun was fired a
second time, giving notice of the *imsâk*, the abstention.
During those two hours, the sleepy Muslimîn rose from
their beds and despatched the last meal which they might

eat before the ensuing sunset. At this early hour the Meccans commonly ate the cold rice and meat left at the evening meal, followed by dates and *finjâns* [cups] of tea. The moment the second gunshot is heard, those who have not finished eating, quickly swallow the last mouthfuls. They then mentally declare their 'intention' of fasting during the ensuing daylight hours. . . .

"Those who have eaten their *sahûr* meal soon after the first gunshot will either lie down to sleep again until the hour of the dawn-prayer (about 4.45 A.M.) or sit to read the Koran aloud. After praying the dawn-prayer in the Haram, the Meccans return to their houses, and enter their private apartments to sleep. The more religious among them read aloud a thirtieth part of the Koran every morning during Ramadân, and thus go completely through the Book during the month. Some read as much as a quarter of the volume (of some three hundred pages) every day —reading the whole some seven times during the month. A person walking in the lanes of Mecca on a Ramadân morning hears voices chanting the Koran in nearly every house. Many do their chanting in the cloisters of the Haram. Thus, with sleeping, reading and praying, the Muslims spend the long slow hours until sunset. . . .

"At the hour of *al-'asr* [the afternoon] a number of shaykhs are usually to be seen sitting in the Haram delivering theological lectures. . . . They perform this voluntary work of preaching in order that they may benefit by the peculiar blessing which is believed to come to one who does good deeds in this, the most holy spot on earth.

"As the hour of sunset approaches, the Mosque becomes ever more crowded, until the pavement beneath the cloisters is almost completely covered with turbaned figures sitting cross-legged on their prayer-mats. Many chant the Koran in an undertone, swaying their bodies from side to side, others sit talking among themselves, or staring at the Ka'ba. Most of them have a small bundle of dates and bread, tied in a handkerchief. Here the famished multitude sits, patiently waiting for sunset. At last the gun booms out from the hill-top of Jiyâd. Instantly a buzzing murmur is heard all over the great quadrangle, of many voices giving praise to God. The handkerchiefs of food, the knots of which have already been loosened, are now spread open; and repeating the brief Muslim word of grace, the ravenous fasters eat a few dates or a piece of bread. Those who have food, gently invite others who sit near them to partake of their fragmentary repast. . . .

"While the members of the assembled multitude are thus relieving their hunger, the *mu'adhdhins* in the minarets are already chanting forth the *adhân* for the sunset prayer. Now all rise, wiping their lips, to perform their devotions. Prayers being over, they quickly disperse to their houses.

"Returning to his house after prayers, the Meccan eats plentifully of a white soup, of wheat broiled in meat broth. This is followed, after an interval of half-an-hour, by the usual dinner-dishes of meat, rice, and vegetables. At this meal, the principal one in the Ramadân day, the Meccan sits for perhaps an hour—eating, drinking tea, and smoking. Later on, he will sit with his cronies until midnight, with an interval for the purpose of performing the *'ishâ'* prayer (between the end of dusk and the passing of one third of the night) in the Haram. Those of a more religious order say long supererogatory prayers during the nights of the second half of this month. Many of the Meccans remain awake, praying or amusing themselves, until the *sahûr* gun is fired." [11]

These prayers or *tarâwîh*, meritorious, but not required, consist generally of twenty *rak'a*, and are performed after the *'ishâ'* prayer. The faithful gather in groups from ten to one hundred and fifty each behind an *imâm*. "The length of the *tarâwîh* varies a good deal: on one spot a group of people has formed who have much to do in the night and whose *imâm* makes the recitation as short as possible and takes only ten to twenty minutes for the twenty parts," (which might normally take about an hour); elsewhere the faithful listen to the recitation of the Koran for the better part of the night. "Amongst the pious 'learned' are many who, though they have in the day time enjoyed only some short, necessary spells of slumber, also, after the *tarâwîh*, so long as may be, exercise themselves in Koran-reciting, chanting, and other voluntary performances: the efforts of these religious heroes, efforts made possible by severe discipline and practice, are truly astounding." [12]

Adding a slight touch of grotesque exaggeration, Burton has graphically portrayed the mood of those exacting Ramadân days: "Like the Italian, the Anglo-Catholic, and the Greek fasts, the chief effect of the 'blessed month' upon True Believers is to darken their tempers into positive gloom. . . . The men curse one another and beat the women. The women slap and abuse the children, and these in their turn cruelly entreat, and use bad language to, the dogs and cats. You can scarcely spend ten minutes in any populous part of the city without hearing some violent dispute. . . . The Mosques are crowded with a sulky, grumbling population, making themselves offensive to one another on earth whilst working their way to heaven." [13]

The relaxation of nightly entertainment—for side by side and almost in competition with intense prayer exercises a number of popular amusements is offered—may to some extent neutralize the tension of the fasting period, but full relief has to wait the end of the month. When Ramadân draws to its close, the population again watches with excited interest for the appearance of the new moon. Will the great celebration of the First of Shawwâl follow on the Twenty-ninth of Ramadân or will the fast have to be extended for another wearying day?

H. St. J. B. Philby, who spent the Ramadân of 1918 in ar-Riyâd, the Wahhâbî capital, gives a lively account of the scene: "Just before sunset . . . there was a great concourse of people assembled on the housetops craning their necks in the direction of the jagged lip of Tuwaiq set off by a sunset of unusual splendor. Many of the crowd were women, who are credited with keener sight than

men, and I had an uncanny feeling that my prediction
(from the Nautical Almanach) of the probable appearance of the moon was known to many of the watchers
who, in spite of the extra day's fast involved, would be
almost glad to have the infidel's impudence confounded
by a manifestation of the divine arbitrariness. And as luck
would have it a band of wispy clouds lay over the moon's
position throughout those critical moments. . . . As the
darkness gathered about us it was clear that the moon
was not to be seen that night, and disappointed figures
crept down from their roofs to break the fast which was
to be endured for another day." At 2 A.M., however, gun-
shots suddenly announced the end of Ramadân. "Some
Bedouin . . . had come in post-haste to report that they
had seen the crescent of the new moon" and an ecclesiastical court had accepted their evidence.[14]

Even when the new moon is announced in a less dramatic manner, the news spreads instantly to the four
corners of the town and the revival of activity, with an
indescribable outburst of noise, is instantaneous. Prepa-
rations have to be rushed for the *'îd as-saghîr*, the Little
Festival, or more properly called, the *'îd al-fitr*, the Festival of Breaking Fast (in Turkish, *küçük bairam* or *şeker
bairam*, small or sugar festival, because of the sweets ex-
changed as presents on this occasion). The "Little"
Festival, since it marks the anticlimax to a period of ex-
hausting devotions is celebrated with much greater enthusiasm and, in fact, is a much more popular feast than
the Great Festival which takes place at the same time as
the sacrifice at Minà. Both are alike as regards their special
prayer services and both as a rule last three to four days.
But the spontaneous cheer of the *'îd al-fitr* has no counter-
part in the somewhat learned and studied exhilaration of
the *'îd al-kabîr*.

"Soon after sunrise on the first day, the people having
all dressed in new or in their best clothes, the men assemble
in the mosques, and perform the prayers of two rak'ahs
. . . after which the khateeb [*khatîb*, or preacher] delivers an exhortation." [15] Such a *khutba*, in which little is

left to the individual orator and the style of which is typical of any sermon, runs somewhat as follows:

"In the name of God, the Compassionate, the Merciful. —Holy is God, who has opened the door of mercy for those who fast and in mercy and kindness has granted them the right of entrance into heaven. God is greater than all. There is no god save Him. . . . Holy is He Who certainly sent the Koran to our Prophet in the month of Ramadân, and who sends angels to grant peace to all true believers. God is great! and worthy of all praise. We praise and thank Him for the *'id al-fitr,* that great blessing, and we testify that beside Him there is no god. He is alone. He has no partner. This witness which we give to His unity will be a cause of our safety here, and finally gain us an entrance to Paradise." After the praise of the Prophet and an exhortation to almsgiving, the preacher usually discusses the merits of Ramadân: "The religious duties of the first ten days of Ramadân gain the mercy of God, those of the second ten merit His pardon; whilst those of the last ten save those who do them from the punishment of Hell." Switching to the excellence of the Koran, sent down to the Prophet, during this month, the *khatîb* concludes: "God has made the fast easy for you. O Believers, God will bless you and us by the grace of the Holy Koran. Every verse of it is a benefit to us and fills us with wisdom. God is the Bestower, the Holy King, the Munificent, the Kind, the Nourisher, the Merciful, the Clement." [16]

"Friends meeting in the mosque, or on the street, or in each other's houses, congratulate and embrace and kiss each other. They generally visit each other for this purpose. Some, even the lower classes, dress themselves entirely in a new suit of clothes; and almost everyone wears something new, if it be only a pair of shoes. The servant is presented with one or more new articles of clothing by the master, and receives a few piasters from each of his master's friends; . . . if he have served a former master, he also visits him, and is in like manner rewarded for his trouble; and sometimes he brings a present of a dish

11. Looking for the new moon at the end of Ramadân.

The poet Mu'izzî (d. 1147/8), who was court poet in the service of Sultan Sanjar (1118-1157), going out with his royal master (first from the left) to see the new moon at the end of the fast of Ramadân. The poet wears a turban; the prince and his followers are represented in Mongol dress. (London, India Office Library, Ethé no. 912, dated 714/1314.)

From Sir T. W. Arnold and A. Grohmann, *The Islamic Book. A Contribution to Its Art and History from the VII-XVIII Century*, Paris, 1929.

12. The Indian Emperor Jahângîr (1605-27) attending mosque at the 'îd al-fitr.

From a ms. in the Berlin State Museum, Islamic Dept. Courtesy of Dr. Richard Ettinghausen.

of sweet cakes, and obtains, in return, money of twice the
value, or more. . . . Most of the shops . . . are closed,
excepting those at which eatables and sherbet are sold;
but the streets present a gay appearance, from the crowds
of passengers in their holiday-clothes."

To Western sentiment, the strangest feature of the
Little as well as of the Great festival is its combination
with a festival of the dead. Most families visit the tombs
of their relatives on this occasion. Palm-branches, broken
into several pieces, are laid on the graves. The family
groups, mostly women, also carry food to distribute to
the poor who throng the cemeteries. Sometimes a tent is
pitched over the grave visited. The *Fâtiha* is said and occasionally the whole Koran is recited by one or more professional "readers." The men leave as soon as the ceremonies are over, but the women stay throughout the day
and may even spend the night in the cemetery, especially
if the family possesses a private and enclosed burial-
ground with a house in it that is equipped for just these
occasions. In Lane's day popular entertainment had in-
vaded some of the cemeteries.

"The great cemetery of Bâb an-Nasr, in the desert
tract immediately on the north of the metropolis [Cairo],
presents a remarkable scene on the two *'id's*. In a part
next to the city-gate from which the burial-ground takes
its name [and which is still standing in our time], many
swings and whirligigs are erected, and several large tents;
in some of which, dancers, reciters [of popular romances],
and other performers, amuse a dense crowd of spectators." [15]

★

iv . The Prophet and the Saints

THE PILGRIMAGE AND THE FASTING DE-
veloped in accordance with the Prophet's intentions. It is
true that the ritualism of the Fast cannot be substantiated
in the Koran; but it constitutes merely a further elaboration, in a sense even a logical outgrowth, of his legalistic
tendencies. On the other hand, the cult of the Prophet
as well as that of the saints represent a striking deviation
from the genuine Prophetic tradition. Its alien character
was clearly realized not only by the occasional reformer
bent on restoring the religious conditions of the age of
the founder, but also at all times by a strong party within
orthodox Islam.

To himself, Muhammad was but the messenger of the
Lord, the executor of His will. He is made of the same
clay as every other man. He will die like every other man.
*Muhammad is only a messenger; before him the messengers
have passed away. If then he dies or is killea, will ye turn
back upon your heels? If anyone turns back upon his
heels, he will not injure Allâh at all* (Koran 3:138). Here
the fact that even Muhammad is not irreplaceable is
clearly expressed. Being human, he is fallible and not exempt from sin. God addresses him: *Say: "If I go astray,
it is to my own disadvantage, and if I let myself be guided,
it is by what my Lord suggests to me; He hears and is
near at hand"* (Koran 34:49). And elsewhere he is ex-
horted: *Seek pardon for thy sins, and for the believers,
male and female* (Koran 47:21).

He is the Lord's spokesman and the preacher of His

truth. He is not able to perform miracles (while Jesus was; Koran 5:109-110). The pagans urged him to give them a sign in proof of his mission. *They say: "We shall not give thee credence till thou causest for us to bubble up from the earth a spring; . . . or until thou causest the heaven to fall upon us in fragments as thou hast said* [in prophesying about the Last Day], *or thou producest Allâh and the angels before our eyes. Or until thou hast a house of ornamental work; or thou ascendest into the heaven, nor shall we give credence to thy ascent until thou bringest down to us a writing which we may read." Say: "Glory be to my Lord! am I anything but a human being* [sent] *as a messenger?"* (Koran 17:92. 94-95). True, every prophet is given a miracle—Moses threw his staff and it turned into a snake; Jesus blew life into a bird of clay—but Muhammad's miracle is the fact of Revelation, the Book itself, a miracle superior to those of his predecessors in that it is permanent while theirs were passing. Consequently, the Prophet must not be made the object of a cult. He will intercede for the faithful on the Day of Judgment, but only *by permission of the Lord.*

Not only did folk-tale and legend, which everywhere tend to raise its heroes to a supernatural level and thereby rob them of the full value of their human achievement, almost immediately upon his death transform him into the familiar type of the semi-divine wonder-worker, but several other factors were more or less independently working to set him up as the object of a cult worship. The abyss which Islam opened between Creator and creature made man look for an intercessor whose authority would be more powerful, if he were less tainted by human frailties. Contact with the Christian churches, as it grew closer after the conquests, brought about a rivalry between religious heroes. It was inconceivable that the central figure of Islam should have been without that supernatural power which, especially to the Christians of the day, seemed so important and so convincing a characteristic of the Chosen of the Lord.

Muhammad had focused the piety of his community on the Lord and the Lord alone. But very soon a tendency could be noted among the faithful to personalize the object of their religious sentiment, to seek the spiritual director of mankind among the living, to bestow their devotion, if perhaps not always their worship, on a human being in whom the Lord's spirit or a spark of His substance was felt to exist.

The Shî'a, growing out of the party that recognized the Prophet's cousin and son-in-law 'Alî (the fourth caliph, assassinated in 661) as the only legitimate heir to Muhammad's temporal position as the political head of his community, considered 'Alî's descendants to be divinely appointed *imâm's*—or leaders. Their leadership was understood to go beyond the merely political claim to the caliphate, which, incidentally, they never attained. They were held to be the inheritors of the direct contact with the Divinity as the Prophet had possessed it, the continuity of which was thus preserved. There was often uncertainty as to which member of the Prophet's family was the *imâm* of his time, but the function of the *imâm* and its indispensability were not questioned. Even when political vicissitudes drove the *imâm* underground in 873, when the incumbent disappeared and was believed to have retired into a mountain, it was not doubted that he would surely return at the suitable moment to claim his rightful position.

The majority of Islam, however, rejected the doctrine and the Shî'a developed into a sectarian movement, frequently persecuted. But the psychological tendency which it represented in extreme form could, within orthodoxy, be satisfied by endowing the Prophet with some of the traits bestowed by the Shî'a upon their *imâm*. The growth of mysticism that began less than two hundred years after the Prophet's death colored the popular conception of Muhammad's personality by modeling it after the great saints of Sûfism, the Muslim variety of mysticism. Around 900 the leader of a conventicle that professed belief in the divinity of the Prophet was executed as a heretic. Yet five hundred years later 'Abdalkarîm al-Jîlî—himself a descendant of the great saint of Baghdad, 'Abdalqâdir al-Kîlânî (d. 1166)—was unopposed when he called Muhammad as the Perfect Man "the preserver of the universe, the pole on which all the spheres of existence revolve," and "the final cause of creation," as well as, at the same time, "the first-created of God and the archetype of all other created beings." The Prophet is "loved and adored as the perfect image or copy of God." He is made to say: "He that has seen me has seen Allâh." [1] It need scarcely be stated that theology had long since articulated popular feeling in recognizing the Prophet's immunity from error and sin.

In chronological terms, the spread of the cult of the saints preceded that of the Prophet. The Koran uses the term *walî*, which means literally: protector, benefactor or friend, and speaks of *the friends of Allâh*, upon whom *rests no fear, nor do they grieve* (Koran 10:63). The Book also singles out some of the pious as *muqarrab*, drawn near to God (Koran 56:11), and *walî* is also applied to the Lord and is one of His names in the Muslim rosary.

From passages of this kind it is concluded "that God has saints, *auliyâ'* [plural of *walî*], whom He has specially distinguished by His friendship and whom He has chosen to be the governors of His kingdom and has marked out to manifest His actions and has peculiarly favòred with diverse kinds of miracles and has purged of natural corruptions and has delivered from subjection to their lower soul and passion, so that all their thoughts are of Him and their intimacy is of Him alone. Such have been in past ages, and are now, and shall be hereafter until the Day of Resurrection, because God has exalted this [Muslim] community above all others and has promised to preserve the religion of Muhammad. . . . God . . . has caused the prophetic evidence to remain down to the present day, and has made the Saints the means whereby it is manifested, in order that the signs of the Truth and the proof of Muhammad's veracity may continue to be clearly seen. He has made the saints the governors of the universe; they have become entirely devoted to His business, and have ceased to follow their sensual affections. Through the blessing of their advent the rain falls from heaven, and through the purity of their lives the plants spring up from the earth, and through their spiritual influence the Muslims gain victories over the unbelievers." [2]

The saints form a hierarchy. The world is never without saints, but who they are need not be known. Nor need every saint be aware of his state. Upon death, they are replaced so that the hierarchy is never incomplete. The highest of the six or seven degrees of sainthood is that of the *qutb*, or pole (also called *ghauth*, or blessing), whose function is to remove any imperfection in the universe that is pointed out to him by the *autâd*, saints of a lower order, who nightly go around the whole world.

The saint, who has been defined as "the one who knows God and His attributes, in so far as it is possible," has the gift of grace, that is of performing miracles, *karâmât*. "The Grace appears on behalf of the *walî* by way of contradicting the customary way of things, such as covering a great distance in a short time and the appearance of food and drink and clothing at the time of need and walking on the water and in the air and such as the speaking of inanimate solid objects and of animals . . . and other things of the same kind." [3] But some saints can do even more; they can transform themselves, speak many tongues, and revive the dead; the *walî* can read thoughts and raise himself from the grave. [4]

Some saints have attempted to place sainthood on a purely moral basis. Of the Persian mystic and poet, Abû Sa'îd b. abî 'l-Khair (d. 1049) the following story is told: "They said to him, 'So-and-so walks on the water.' He replied: 'It is easy enough: frogs and water-fowl do it.' They said, 'So-and-so flies in the air.' 'So do birds and insects,' he replied. They said, 'So-and-so goes from one town to another in a moment of time.' 'Satan,' he rejoined, 'goes in one moment from the East to the West. Things like these have no great value.' And he added: 'The true saint goes in and out amongst the people and eats and sleeps with them and buys and sells in the market and marries and takes part in social intercourse, and never forgets God for a single moment.' " [5] But he could not prevent his followers from reporting that all manner of miracles had been performed by him.

Since Islam has set up no authority to investigate and determine the claim of a devotee to be worshiped as a saint, it is public opinion that bestows the status of *walî* on an individual. Saints, thus, have tended to become very numerous, and at the same time rather restricted in the geographical range of their cult. Their origins vary widely. "Some are great mystics, often founders of orders or of religious brotherhoods; others are ancestors or chiefs of tribes, princes and founders of dynasties. Some are of humbler origin, *illuminati*, half-deranged persons, *majdhûb*, whose peculiar or incoherent utterances are often regarded as inspired, or even the simple-minded. Other saints are transformations or survivals of old days, gods of woods and springs; . . . As in the Roman Catholic worship, saints are patrons of towns, villages, trades and corporations." [6]

In regulating the cult of the saints, orthodox theology was mainly concerned with safeguarding the precedence of the Prophet over the *walî*. A miracle attributed to the Prophet was neatly distinguished from the saint's *karâma* by the explanation that it was Allâh who brought it about to demonstrate the sincerity of His messenger so that His ultimate purpose—the salvation of men through the apostle's preaching—be furthered. But as to the actual devotional practices, the theologians were much less reluctant to sanction them or at least to accept them tacitly, than they were to condone or justify the cult of the Prophet. As happened not infrequently in Islam, the intellectual and the emotional centers of personal religion could only be made to converge slowly, without ever quite coinciding.

It seems that the tomb of the Prophet in Medina attracted the pious attention of visitors earlier than the house of his birth in the modern Sûq al-Lail in Mecca. Even now the pilgrimage to his tomb in Medina remains an almost customary sequel to the *hajj*, whereas his birthplace, first transformed into a place of prayer by Khaizurân (d. 789/90), the mother of the caliph Hârûn ar-Rashîd (786-809), is accorded less attention. Muhammad died on Monday, the twelfth of the First Rabî' and his birthday, the date of which is not known, has been arbitrarily placed on the same date. The sources are silent as to when his birthday, *maulid* (mostly pronounced *môlid*) was first honored by a public celebration. Ibn Jubair (late twelfth century) has reference to such a celebration, also called *maulid*, as to an established custom.[7] Perhaps a century earlier, the Egyptian government tried unsuccessfully to prohibit the processions of palace dignitaries, at which several *khutbas* (sermons) marked the *maulid an-nabî*—the birthday of the Prophet—or else that of 'Alî, Fâtima (the Prophet's daughter and 'Alî's wife), and even that of the reigning caliph. It should be noted that the *maulid* was not at this time a festival of the people, but a ceremony performed by the Shî'ite groups that were in control of the country.

According to the Sunnite historians and theologians, the first *maulid* celebration is that arranged by Muzaffar ad-Din Kökbürü, a brother-in-law of the famed Saladin, which took place in Arbela, southeast of Mosul in Upper Mesopotamia, in the year 1207. In this festival those Sûfî and Christian influences are prominent which, together with the tendencies represented by the Shî'a, have done so much toward the development of the veneration of the Prophet and the saints. In a splendid passage the great historian, Ibn Khallikân (d. 1282), himself a native of Arbela, describes Kökbürü's *maulid:*

"The pomp with which [the prince] celebrated the birthday of the Prophet surpassed all description; I shall, however, give a feeble outline of the ceremony. The people of the neighboring provinces, having heard what veneration he testified to the Prophet, hastened to Arbela every year, and an immense multitude of jurisconsults, sûfîs, preachers, Koranreaders, and poets arrived there, at the same time, from Baghdad, Mosul, Mesopotamia, Sinjâr, Nasîbîn, Persian 'Irâq, and all the other places in the vicinity. The influx of strangers continued without interruption from the month of Muharram [the first of the year] till the commencement of the First Rabî' [the third month]. Already, by his orders, upwards of twenty wooden pavilions, divided into four or five stories, were erected, one being appropriated to himself and each of the others to an emir or some person holding a high rank in the state. On the first day of the month of Safar [the second month], these pavilions were decorated in a most splendid manner; a choir of singers, a band of musicians, and a troop of exhibitors of Chinese shadows were established in each; not a story being left without a company of these artists. During the whole period all business remained suspended, and the sole occupation of the people was to amuse themselves and walk from one band to another. These pavilions were erected on a line from the gate of the citadel to the entrance of the [Sûfî] convent near the hippodrome [previously built by Kökbürü], and every day, after the *'asr* [afternoon] prayer, Muzaffar ad-Dîn went forth and stopped at each pavilion successively; listening to the music, and amusing himself with looking at the Chinese shadows or whatever else might be going on. He then passed the night in the convent, listening to religious music, and the next morning, after the prayer, he rode out to hunt, and returned to the citadel before the hour of noon. He continued in the same practice, every day, till the eve of the anniversary, and this he celebrated, one year on the eighth day of the month, and the next on the twelfth, in consequence of the different opinions held respecting the true date. Two days previously to the anniversary, he sent an immense flock of camels, oxen, and sheep to the hippodrome, accompanied with all his drummers, singers, and musicians. These animals were there sacrificed as victims, and a number of cauldrons being set up, the flesh was cooked in various manners. On the eve of the anniversary, after the sunset

74

prayer, he listened to a concert in the citadel, and then went forth, preceded by a great number of persons bearing wax-lights. Two, or four of these lights, I am not sure of the exact number, were such as are employed in the grand ceremonies, being fastened, each of them, on the back of a mule, with a man seated behind to support it. He advanced in this manner to the convent, and the next day, at an early hour, a quantity of pelisses were brought out of the establishment by the Sûfîs, each of them bearing a bundle of them in each hand, and advancing one after another. A great number of these dresses, I do not know exactly how many, having been brought out, he went down to the convent, where the persons of high distinction, the chiefs, and a great number of other eminent individuals had already assembled. A chair was then placed for the preacher, and Muzaffar ad-Dîn went up into a wooden tower, erected to receive him. This edifice had windows overlooking the place where the assembly and the preacher were, and another set of windows opened on the hippodrome which was extremely wide. There, the soldiery were collected in a body, and the prince passed them in review, now looking at them, and then at the public and the preacher. When the soldiers had all defiled successively, a repast was brought into the hippodrome for the poor; a public repast, consisting of an immense quantity of meat and bread. Another repast was prepared in the convent for the persons who had attended the preaching. Whilst the troops were defiling and the preachers exhorting, he sent for all the chiefs and eminent men, and for the doctors, preachers, Koranreaders, and poets, who had come from the neighboring countries to witness the solemnity; each of these persons was separately introduced and clothed in a pelisse, after which he returned to his place. When all had been presented, the repast was brought in, and a portion of it was sent to the house of such of the company, as were judged worthy of the honor. Toward the hour of the *'asr* prayer, or somewhat later, the repast ended, and the prince passed that night in the convent, listening to religious concerts till day-break.

Such was his custom every year, . . . When the solemnity was ended, all prepared for their departure, and every one of them received from him a donation." [8]

With the growth of Sûfism in Egypt, the *maulid* took root there and thence spread in a comparatively short time all through the Muslim world. The theologians were hesitant. The deepening of the reverence for the Prophet could only be encouraged and, in Islam, consensus is recognized as making law. On the other hand, the celebration clearly was *bid'a*, an innovation, running counter both to dogmatic theory and traditional practice. One of the intellectual ancestors of Wahhâbism, Ibn Taimiyya (d. 1328), in a *fatwà* (legal opinion) tersely condemns the introduction of new festivals such as that celebrated "during one of the nights of the First Rabî', alleged to be the night of the birth of the Prophet." [9] The participation of women was criticized with especial vigor by his contemporary, Ibn al-Hâjj (d. 1336), and it still gives occasional offense to the more strict-minded and orthodox. Suyûtî (d. 1505) discussed the question at length and voiced the prevailing opinion of his own and subsequent times in arriving at the conclusion that the celebration was indeed an "innovation," but a praiseworthy one—*bid'a hasana*. The picture he draws of the *maulid* differs somewhat from Ibn Khallikân's and comes fairly close to present usage.

Suyûtî considers the recitation of the Koran and of the "histories" of the Prophet—often in verse or in a combination of prose and poetry—the core of the celebration, and the processions, feasting, and fairs mere accessories.[10] These panegyrics, also called *maulid's*, which may originally have been inspired by the sermon usual at festivals of Christian saints, trace the major events of the Prophet's life, emphasizing its miraculous character, and dwell reverently and extravagantly on his *manâqib*, or virtues. The *maulid* poems, of which there are a great many in both Arabic and Turkish, have attained to such popularity that they have come to be recited on other festive occasions as well. For instance, it has become pious practice in Mecca to have a *maulid* recited by professional readers on the seventh day after the death of a near relative. In Palestine *maulids* are often recited in fulfillment of a religious vow.[11]

The Sûfî contribution to the popularization of the *maulid* celebration is attested by the fact that in Egypt, where the *maulid* procession is witnessed by the king or his representative, the *maulid* proper is accompanied by so-called *dhikr*-meetings. *Dhikr*, the remembrance or glorification of God with certain fixed phrases, repeated in ritual order and coordinated with movements or a peculiar breathing technique, is an integral part of the ritual of all the Sûfî, or dervish, fraternities. The purpose of the practice is to induce an ecstatic experience of the closeness of the Lord or of momentary union with Him. The actual sequence of phrases and motions varies from order to order, and much is left to the inspiration of the presiding shaikh. But the pattern is everywhere the same. Formulae such as "There is no god but Allâh," or "God is greatest," or the several names of Allâh, are repeated innumerable times in a certain rhythm. Songs may be added with drums and pipes used as accompaniment. The *dhikr* meetings are held frequently, sometimes nightly, and at least once a week they accompany the regular Friday service in the house of the order. Their integration in the *maulid* shows better than anything else the extent to which Sûfî piety has become representative of popular religious feeling.

The shyness and embarrassment with which the strict theologians and most of the modern intellectuals confront the delicate problem of finding the right balance between indifference to and "idolatrous" worship of the Prophet is reflected by a *fatwà* of Ibn Taimiyya. Ibn Taimiyya tried, without obtaining much response outside of Wahhâbî and some modernistic circles, to define permissible reverence as against blameworthy adoration. In discussing the ritual to be observed when approaching Muhammad's tomb in the Mosque of the Prophet in Medina, Ibn Taimiyya directs: "When the Muslim enters Medina let him repair to

the Mosque of the Prophet and there pray; for one prayer
in this mosque is better than a thousand in any other, save
only the Haram of Mecca. Let him then salute the Prophet
. . . ; for of a truth he said: 'If any man salute me, verily
Allâh will give back my spirit unto me, that I may return
his salutation.' . . . According to the majority of the
learned . . . it is correct for the visitor to face the tomb,
that is, to stand with his back turned towards the *qibla*.
. . . All authorities agree that the visitor must not touch
nor kiss the tomb-chamber, nor circumambulate it, nor
pray towards it. And if the visitor says in his salutation
'Peace be upon thee, O Messenger of Allâh! O Prophet of
Allâh! O Best of Allâh's created beings! O Most Honored
by thy Lord of all creation! O Leader of the Pious Ones!':
if he says this, then he has said all, for these are all the
attributes which are his—Allâh bless him and give him
peace! Let him offer up no supplication as he stands over
against the tomb. . . . Verily, the Prophet said: 'O God!
Let not my tomb become an idol that is worshipped!' " [12]

Renan, the great French historian and philosopher,
states that "men have since their beginnings worshipped
at the same places"; this probably needs to be qualified in
the sense that "the continuance of their vogue as religious
centers depends on the continuance of their population
and is materially aided by the establishment in them of
religious orders and consequent organisations." [13] The
continuity of the cults is thus interrupted less often in
Egypt, Syria or Palestine than, say, in Asia Minor where
Islam came in spearheaded by new population strata, the
Seljuq and later the Ottoman Turks. In Asia Minor, therefore, more sanctuaries survived the change from paganism
to Christianity than that from Christianity to Islam. In
Palestine, on the other hand, rededications like that of the
cave on the Mount of Olives are fairly typical. This cave
now "honored by the Mohammedans as the shrine of
Râbi'a 'l-'Adawiyya (d. 801) was revered by the Christians as the place where Pelagia atoned for her sins, while

the Jews cherish the still older belief that this place is the shrine of the prophetess Khuldah." [14]

As is to be expected, primitive forms of worship and primitive concepts of who is to be worshipped will linger at such local sanctuaries and the practical religion of the unlettered will conform only in very general terms to the doctrines of Islam. The local tradition often makes its peace with Islam by assigning its sacred tree or stone to a saint who is identified with a Koranic figure or by recognizing the saint as a *nabî* or prophet. This is all the easier done, for neither the Book nor orthodox tradition offer a complete listing of divine messengers. The result of this incomplete integration of ancient places of worship into Islam is that they are visited by the Christian section of the population as well and, in turn, Muslim devotees have no compunction about invoking the aid of the local saint of the Christians. The miracles of the saints cut across denominational lines, while their various activities and the forms of their cults may well perpetuate with but slight modifications the service expected from, and offered to, them, in an even remoter past.

Sir Arthur Evans' description of the cult of a minor Muslim saint's sanctuary at Tekke Keui (near Usküb in Southern Serbia) illustrates the religious situation to perfection. "Taking his stand on the flat stone by the pillar, the suppliant utters a prayer for what he most wishes, and afterwards embraces the stone in such a way that the finger tips meet at its further side. . . . The worshipper who would conform to the full ritual, now fills a keg of water from a spring that rises near the shrine—another primitive touch—and makes his way through a thorny grove up a neighboring knoll, on which is a wooden enclosure surrounding a Mohammedan Saint's Grave or Tekke. Over the headstone of this grows a thorn tree hung with rags of divers colours, attached to it—according to a widespread primitive rite—by sick persons who had made pilgrimage to the tomb. . . . In the centre of the grave was a hole, into which the water from the holy spring was poured, and mixed with the holy earth. Of this the votary drinks three times, and he must thrice anoint his forehead with it. . . .

"It was now necessary to walk three times round the grave, each time kissing and touching with the forehead the stone at the head and foot of it. A handful of the grave dust was next given me, to be made up into a triangular amulet and worn round the neck. An augury of pebbles, which were shuffled about under the Dervish's palms over a hollowed stone, having turned out propitious, we now proceeded to the sacrifice. This took place outside the sepulchral enclosure, where the Priest of the Stone was presently ready with a young ram. My Albanian guide cut its throat, and I was now instructed to dip my right hand little finger in the blood and to touch my forehead with it.

"The sacrifice completed, we made our way down again to the shrine . . . it was now necessary to divest one's self of an article of clothing for the Dervish to wrap around the sacred pillar, where it remained all night. Due offerings of candles were made, which, as evening drew on, were lit on the sunken hearth beside the stone. We were given three barley corns to eat, and a share in the slaughtered ram, of which the rest was taken by the priest, was set apart for our supper in the adjoining antechamber. Here, beneath the same roof with the stone, and within sight of it through the open doorway, we were bidden to pass the night, so that the occult influences due to its spiritual possession might shape our dreams as in the days of the patriarchs." [15]

The saint may be male or female; in fact, some of the female saints like Sitta Nefîsa and Sayyida Zainab in Cairo enjoy considerable importance in the devotional life of the population. Occasionally, the service of the saint is confined to women worshippers, as is that of Shaikh Mahmûd in Mecca.

The day especially set aside in honor of the saint is usually believed to be his birthday or perhaps even more frequently that of his death when he was, as it were, born into eternal life. In other cases, his festival is not a *maulid*,

13. Mosque scene.

The central structure illustrates the tower erected by Kökbürü. To the left, a preacher on the pulpit, addressing the congregation. To the right, the fountain. The Persian mosques are "open-air courts with buildings around them, a minaret and a high arch marking the prayer-niche" oriented toward Mecca.

This miniature, painted by Bihzâd in 1529, portrays a different incident from that described by Ibn Khallikân, but suggests very well the setting of Kökbürü's *mawlid* celebration.

14. The Mystic Dance of a Sûfî fraternity.

By Muhammadî of Herât; Iran, middle of sixteenth century.
Courtesy of the Smithsonian Institution, Freer Gallery of Art,
Washington, D.C.

or anniversary celebration, but a *mausim* (literally: sea-son—of celebrating a fair or a feast), the timing of which may reflect that of an ancient nature festival rather than an event in the more or less legendary life of the saint him-self. Depending on the standing of the saint, this *mausim* may be confined to a single day or spread over three or four. Thus, the famous Feast of Nebî Mûsà (Moses), which in its main features is typical of all such celebra-tions, extends from the Friday preceding Good Friday (ac-cording to the calendar of the Greek Orthodox Church) through Maundy Thursday.

The shrine of Nebî Mûsà is located four miles southwest of Jericho, just off the Jerusalem road. His establishment is divided into the sanctuary proper, which is built over the supposed grave of the prophet, and surrounding rooms separated from the sanctuary by an open courtyard. These rooms serve mostly for the accommodation of visitors. Kitchens, stables, and storerooms are attached to the estab-lishment, which also contains two mosques and a ceme-tery, for it is counted a blessing to be interred near the prophet.

The procession begins in Jerusalem when the banner of Nebî Mûsà is handed to the Muftî, who unfolds it and has it fastened to a stick. "The banner is made of green velvet, embroidered along the border with golden threads; a piece of black silk is sewn at the center of each side bearing" inscriptions. The procession (which in Turkish days used to be accompanied by a military band and a guard of honor) slowly moves out of Jerusalem, led by the Muftî, the banner-bearer, and the servants of the prophet. Every-where the streets are filled with spectators who carry the flags of other local saints. From a certain point, the jour-ney may be continued by car or carriage. The official pro-cession is not the only one that reaches Nebî Mûsà for the *mausim*, but they all resemble each other in their organ-ization.

"The banner-bearer goes ahead, followed by the musi-cians. Then follow some young men of the party, encir-cling their leader and dancing according to the tempo given by him. Every dance is accompanied by singing. The leader recites a strophe and the others repeat it. He swings a sword, a stick or a handkerchief in the air and dances with them, thus giving the tempo. . . . While singing and dancing the party clap their hands in a rhythmical way."

As has often been pointed out, this type of procession bears close resemblance to the joyful processions described in the Bible, as when the Lord threatened the Ammonites for having clapped their hands, stamped their feet and rejoiced in heart against the land Israel (Ezekiel 25:6).

The "servants of the prophet" are recruited from four families. Their functions do not, however, have any priestly or otherwise religious tinge. Two of the families are responsible for the preparation of the food, a third presents the banner-bearers and the fourth the *mu'adhdhin*. The animals are killed while a special formula, rather than the usual "In the name of God," is pronounced over them: "From Thee to Thee [O God] may it be counted as recompense and reward for our lord Mûsà [Moses]." This may be followed by: "Accept your vow, O Interlocutor of God [Moses]." The meat is distributed among those present or else prepared in one of the kitchens. The expenses are met by the income from the endowment, *waqf*, of the prophet. Of privately sacrificed victims, the offerer keeps the larger part for himself and his friends. The *mausim* attracts tradesmen and entertainers. A regular fair is held in the courtyard. Outside, temporary coffee-shops are rigged up; a shadow theater gives performances and horse-races are held. Special *dhikr* meetings are arranged. The recitation of the Koran is listened to in dead silence. With games, songs and ceremonies, the days pass fast and pleasantly. The mood of the visitors is well expressed in this song:

The marriage festival is not a (real) joy,
Nor (is that of) the circumcision of boys;
There is no (real) joy except visiting Moses—
Peace and prayer be upon him.

If it was not you, O Moses, we would not have come and taken
   this trouble,
And we would not have treaded the small stones and the sand
   with our feet.
Good evening, O Moses, O son of 'Imrân.
Thou who livest in the Jordan valley and in Haurân.

The ceremonies in Moses' honor recall Ibn al-Hâjj's pro-
test against the singing and dancing at Abraham's grave in
Hebron as a scandalous innovation.

On Maundy Thursday the official procession with the
banner of Nebî Mûsà returns. The entry into Jerusalem is
accompanied by the same performances that had marked
its departure. On Good Friday, a banner march, without
dancing or music, brings the solemnities to a close.[16]

In certain parts of the Islamic world, Palestine, for example, it has become customary to connect a purely private ceremony such as circumcision with a visit to a saint,
especially Nebî Mûsà. Circumcision which, incidentally, is
not ruled obligatory by all law schools, but nevertheless
has become in the popular mind, together with abstention
from pork, an essential distinction of the true believer,
takes place in the precinct of the sanctuary. The boy is
taken there, accompanied by a procession in which professional dancers and musicians perform and the crowd
sings enthusiastically.

In Mecca as well as in Egypt similar processions are
arranged, but the private character of the occasion is
strictly preserved. Everywhere the boy is dressed as richly
as possible and precautions against the evil eye are taken,
which in Egypt include his being disguised as a girl so as
to mislead the malignant spirits. In North Africa the operation has to be performed with a stone knife, an archaic
survival reminiscent of the passage in Joshua, ch. 5, where
the children of Israel are circumcised with stone instruments upon entering the Holy Land. The other "private"
ceremony of the Muslims, the so-called *'aqîqa*-sacrifice,
which is offered on the seventh day after the birth of a

child, does not seem ever to be tied to the cult of a saint. It is recommended by tradition to name the child on this day and to clip his hair, also called *'aqîqa*, the weight of which in gold or in silver should be given to the poor who also receive the major part of the sacrificial victim's flesh.

★

v · The Tenth of Muharram

SHÎ'ISM, WIDELY REPRESENTED IN IRAQ AND
India and the state religion of Iran and the Yemen, differs
from Sunnism, the so-called orthodox Islam, both in its
emotional atmosphere and in its principal intellectual mo-
tivations. The religious sensibilities are keener, emotional
responses to doctrine more intense, exclusivism and fa-
naticism closer to the surface than in Sunnî Islam where
profound conviction is often accompanied by tolerant
moderation. The inclination of Shî'ism to theological ex-
tremism may have weakened during the last centuries,
when persecution ceased, but the nervous climate of the
Shî'a is still that of a suppressed sect, even where not only
political recognition but political sovereignty has been
achieved.

The first of the two ideas that were added by the Shî'a
to the original message of Islam is the belief in divine
manifestation in man, or more specifically in 'Alî and his
descendants. The bearer of the "divine light" is the *imâm*
of the community, its spiritual and political leader. It is
only through adherence to him that the believer can be
saved. "Whosoever dies without knowing the true *imâm*
of his time, dies the death of an unbeliever." It may be that
some of Muhammad's contemporaries already associated
such ideas with him; it is certain that 'Alî was so regarded
by a section of his followers. The phrase is used: "I seek
God and the future state through my love to 'Alî." In
recent theological formulation the *imâms* are defined as
"immaculate, innocent of any sin, small or great, co-equal,

endowed with every virtue, knowledge and power." And
"all blessings and all knowledge of God come through
them; through them the universe lives and moves and has
its being." [1]

The other idea is that of "the passion" or of vicarious
suffering and it is this that has principally determined the
mood of the Shî'a. It was, however, not the assassination
of 'Alî but the tragedy of Kerbela that provided the indispensable personalization of the idea. On the Tenth of
Muharram, 61 A.H. (October 10, 680), Husain, son of 'Alî
and grandson of the Prophet, who came to be counted as
the third *imâm*, was killed in a skirmish between government troops and a small body of supporters who were ac-
companying him to Kûfa, in Iraq, where his followers had
invited him to lead them in a revolt against the Umayyad
caliphs of Damascus. His grave on the battlefield, about
sixty miles southwest of Baghdad, almost immediately became a goal for pilgrims. And just as swiftly Husain's
death was interpreted as voluntary self-sacrifice—so that it
is through his suffering that the believers enter Paradise.
Husain's fate has created a pattern of martyrdom and
Shî'ite legend represents all its Alid heroes as martyrs who
met their end for the most part by poison at the instigation
of the caliphs. In the words of the poet Muhtasham (d.
1588):

*When they summoned mankind to the table of sorrow, they
first issued the summons to the hierarchy of the Prophets.
When it came to the turn of the Saints, Heaven trembled at
the blow which they smote at the head of the Lion of
God* ['Alî] [2]

It cannot be too strongly emphasized how foreign this concept of salvation by intervention is to Islam as preached
by Muhammad. Its intrusion cannot be ascribed to an
Iranian reaction to Arab doctrines, for the early Shî'ites
were either of Arab descent or Arabicized scripturaries.

As early as 850 or 851, the Caliph Mutawakkil found it
politically necessary to level Husain's tomb and to prohibit pilgrimages to Kerbela. But government intervention

proved of little effect and the rebuilt grave has remained
to this day the devotional center for pilgrims from all over
the Shî'a world. Those that are buried by the sanctuary
will surely enter Paradise. Many aged Shî'î settle in Kerbela or ask in their will to have their bodies transported to
the holy city. For centuries endless caravans of the dead
have been coming into Kerbela from Persia and India,
transforming the town into one vast burial-ground.

It would be incorrect to say that Husain stands in the
center of Shî'a dogma, but it is unquestionably true that
contemplation of his personality and fate is the emotional
mainspring of the believers' religious experience. The principal and most characteristic festival of the Shî'a is built
around his death, which has made him, in the phrase of an
early mourner, "the bond of reconciliation with God on
the Day of Judgment." [3]

Toward the end of the Muslim year, black tents are
pitched in the streets. These tents are adorned with dra-
peries, arms and candelabra. Here and there wooden pulpits are erected. On the first of Muharram, when the festival proper begins, mourning clothes are donned; people
refrain from shaving and bathing, and a simple diet is
adopted. From the pulpit the beginning of Husain's story
is narrated with as much detail and elaboration of episodes
as possible. The listeners are deeply affected. Their cries
of "O, Husain, O, Husain!" are accompanied by groans
and tears. This kind of recitation continues throughout
the day, the mullahs taking turns on the several pulpits.
At one time the notables of a quarter would fit out a tent
and pay a mullah to recite in it, while the listeners were
served food and drink. During the first nine days of
Muharram groups of men, with their half-naked bodies
dyed black or red, tour the streets. They pull out their
hair, inflict sword wounds upon themselves or drag chains
behind them, or perform wild dances. Not infrequently
fights with Sunnites or other adversaries will develop,
resulting in casualties and even deaths.

The celebration culminates on the Tenth of Muharram

in a big procession originally designed as a funerary parade to reenact the burial of Husain. The center of this procession is formed by the coffin of Husain, carried by eight men and accompanied on each side by a banner-bearer. Four horses and some sixty blood-smeared men march behind the coffin and sing a martial tune. They are followed by a horse, representing Duldul, the war-horse of Husain. In the rear there is usually a group of perhaps fifty men rhythmically beating two wooden staves, one against the other.[4]

The poet Qâ'ânî (d. 1853) has given dramatic expression to the thoughts and feelings of the Shî'ites in his catechism-like elegy on the death of Husain. The poem begins:

What rains down? Blood! Who? The Eye! How? Day and Night! Why?

From grief! What grief? The grief of the Monarch of Kerbela! What was his name? Husain! Of whose race? 'Alî's!

Who was his mother? Fâtima! Who was his grandsire? Mustafâ [Muhammad]!

How was it with him? He fell a martyr! Where? In the plain of Mâriya!

When? On the tenth of Muharram! Secretly? No, in public!

Was he slain by night? No, by day! At what time? At noon-tide!

Was his head severed from the throat? No, from the nape of the neck!

Was he slain unthirsting? No! Did none give him to drink? They did!

Who? Shimr! From what source? From the source of death! [5]

It has been pointed out that this ritual, which is without parallel in Islam where a saint is never commemorated by a re-enactment of his funeral, incorporates rites of an earlier cult. A number of details regarding the arrangement and the symbolism of the procession corroborate the general parallelism of the ceremony with the festival of Adonis-Tammuz. The violent death of that god on the approach of summer, symbolizing the decline of nature's productive force under the searing rays of a merciless sun, was followed by a mourning of seven days after which the body was washed, anointed and shrouded to be carried abroad in a procession and finally interred.[6] The fact that the Husain festival did not originate in Persia, but in Mesopotamia where as far as we know the first Tenth of Muharram procession with "solemn wailings and lamentations" was held in 962, localizes it in the region where in various disguises the Adonis tradition was to show some sporadic vitality more than two centuries later. The historian Ibn al-Athîr (d. 1234) records that in 1064 A.D. "a mysterious threat was circulated from Armenia to Khuzistan, that every town which did not lament the dead King of the Jinn should utterly perish." In 1204, the same writer tells us, an epidemic ravaged Mosul and Iraq, "and it was divulged that a woman of the Jinn, called Umm 'Unqûd [Mother of the Grape-Cluster] had lost her son, and that every one who would not make lamentation for him would fall a victim to the epidemic." [7]

While the Tenth of Muharram procession remained confined to the Shî'ite world, the veneration of Husain has spread into Sunnism. The Fâtimids (969–1171) had Husain's head transferred to Cairo and the Mosque of the Hasanain (literally: of the two Hasan—that is, Hasan and his brother Husain) was erected over the relic and still preserves a reputation of especial sanctity. While the mourners in the Shî'a procession are all men, the crowd that assembles in the Hasanain Mosque on the occasion of *'Ashûrâ* is composed almost exclusively of women who gather apparently in order to witness a *dhikr* meeting.[8]

At a comparatively recent date—it was first witnessed by a European in 1811—the *ta'ziya*, or Passion play, the only drama to be developed in either Persian or Arabic literature, became the real climax of the Shî'ite Tenth of Muharram celebrations. The stage requires few properties besides a large *tâbût* (coffin), "receptacles in front to hold lights," and Husain's arms and banner. The poet speaks the introduction and, supported by a choir of boys, chants a *khutba*-like lamentation. Another male choir, dressed as mourning women, utters the wailing of the women and mothers. The spectators are given cakes of earth from Kerbela, steeped in musk, "on which they press their foreheads in abject grief." To defray the expense for a *ta'ziya* is a meritorious work, with which the donor "builds himself the palace in Paradise." [9]

The play consists of a loose sequence of some forty to fifty scenes. Dramatic suspense would be absent even if the events were not known to the audience, for they are foretold by Gabriel to the prophets, foreseen in dreams, and frequently narrated at length before being acted on the stage. The performance is highly realistic, especially in the portrayal of Husain's sufferings from thirst and in the battle and death episodes. Old Testament figures are introduced to typify the events of Husain's Passion. National animosity against the Arabs expresses itself on occasion, but the true villains are Caliph Yazîd, who gives the order to kill Husain, and Shammar, or Shimr, who is believed to have struck the fatal blow.

The excitement of the audience reaches such a pitch that the spectators not infrequently try to lynch the actors representing the murderers of Husain. Anti-Sunnite feeling is said to be such that no Sunnî would be knowingly tolerated among the spectators. The final scenes usually depict the progress of the martyr's severed head to the Court of the Caliph. On the way, the cortège halts at a Christian monastery whose abbot, upon the sight of the head, swears off his faith and professes Islam. The sight of the head produces the same effect on some Christian ambassadors who happen to be at the Court of Yazîd when it arrives. Not only Christians, but Jews and pagans are affected in the same way; even a lion is seen to bow low before Husain's head.

The frequently crude and cruel plays must not blind one to the fact that essentially those *ta'ziyât* are dramatized dogmatics. Theological sayings of the heroes of the faith are constantly quoted. But what is more important is that the idea of salvation through the sacrificial death of

Husain is expounded with great clarity and emphasis. At the very beginning of one of the plays, Gabriel (who here has Hasan share his brother's fate) announces to Muhammad: "Thy two grandchildren shall fall under the blows of a very contemptible enemy, not because they have in some way transgressed God's laws; no, the filth of sin has never soiled a member of thy family, O Phoenix of the Universe! Rather are they sacrificed for the salvation of the people who adopt Islam so that the brow of the martyrs shall eternally reflect the brilliance of the elect of God. If thou desirest the forgiveness of sins of these evil-doing peoples, do not oppose the two roses of thy garden being plucked before the time." [10]

When the government troops have closed in on Husain, after endless conversations in his camp and after he has declined the assistance of the King of the Jinn, the Umayyad general asks for a volunteer to kill the Prophet's grandson. Shimr responds, saying:

"I am he whose dagger is famous for bloodshed. My mother has borne me for this work alone. I care not about the conflict of the Day of Judgment; I am a worshipper of Yazîd [the Umayyad caliph], and have no fear of God. I can make the great throne of the Lord to shake and tremble. I alone can sever from the body the head of Husain the son of 'Alî. I am he who has no share in Islam. I will strike the chest of Husain, the ark of God's knowledge, with my boots, without any fear of punishment.

"*Husain:* Oh, how wounds caused by arrows and daggers do smart! O God, have mercy in the Day of Judgment on my people for my sake. The time of death has arrived, but I have not my Akbar [his son, killed previously] with me. Would to God my grandfather the Prophet were now here to see me!

"*The Prophet* (appearing): Dear Husain, thy grandfather the Prophet of God has come to see thee. I am here to behold the mortal wounds of thy delicate body. Dear child, thou hast at length suffered martyrdom by the cruel hand of my own people! This was the reward I expected from them; thanks be to God! Open thine eyes, dear son, and behold thy grandfather with dishevelled hair. If thou hast any desire in thy heart, speak it out to me.

"*Husain:* Dear grandfather, I abhor life; I would rather go and visit my dear ones in the next world. I earnestly desire to see my companions and friends—above all, my dearly beloved son 'Alî Akbar.

"*The Prophet:* Be not grieved that 'Alî Akbar thy son was killed, since it tends to the good of my sinful people on the day of universal gathering.

"*Husain:* Seeing 'Alî Akbar's martyrdom contributes to the happiness of thy people, seeing my own sufferings give validity to thy office of mediation, and seeing thy rest consists in my being troubled in this way, I would offer my soul, not once or twice, but a thousand times, for the salvation of thy people!

"*The Prophet:* Sorrow not, dear grandchild; thou shalt be a mediator, too, in that day. At present thou art thirsty, but tomorrow thou shalt be the distributor of the water of al-Kausar [in Paradise]."

In this manner the incident of Kerbela is interpreted as an action of cosmic significance. As a Passion play, it is strongly reminiscent of the death of Christ.

The last scene transports us to the Day of Resurrection. Prophets and sinners arise from their graves.

"*The Scribe* (to the sinners): O ye multitudes struck dumb with astonishment, ye silent images, ye who are bound with fetters, chains, and yokes, why did you enslave yourselves to your lust and passions? Why did you sell your goods to men with light weights? Come, O Keeper, take these and carry them off; take vengeance on them in the unquenchable fire.

"*The Sinners:* O God's Messenger, we pray thee to remember us with favor, we are wasting away; run, thou, and save us! We are tormented, we are companions of sorrow, we are in great affliction. Though we are sinners, we are surely thy people?

"*The Prophet:* O great God, have mercy on the sins of my people. Have mercy, O Lord, for I am most terribly distressed and anxious. O God, graciously kindle a torch of mercy, and, in Thy goodness, prevent my people from being burnt in yonder flames.

"*Gabriel:* Withdraw from the people of disobedience, O Prophet of the Lord. Abandon these wretches, and talk no more of them; they are only fit to be eternally destroyed. Go thou to thy place, for it is time God's justice should be made manifest.

"*The Prophet:* How can I bear to remain quiet, O Gabriel? How can I see my beloved followers in such a state? I will rend my garment, and not be ashamed thereat. O Gabriel, I pray thee to let me know what is best to be done.

"*Gabriel:* Hear my statements, O object and desire of all endowed with understanding. If thou intendest to solve this difficulty thou must order Husain to come from Kerbela, for he alone can raise the feet of sinners from the mud of destruction. Should that Noah come and act as pilot of this ship, I have no doubt it will pass safely through the shoreless ocean."

Husain appears in an unforgiving mood. He demands vengeance for the torments inflicted on his family and dwells at length on the tortures each of them has had to suffer.

"*The Prophet:* Oh! what troubles thou must have undergone, O Husain! Who is able to hear such a sad story? Martyrdom is indeed thy crown; trials bring thee near to God and establish a close union between Him and thee. Think not about thy former trials. Let the tree of intercession bear fruit, and bestir thyself now on behalf of the sinners amongst my people.

"*Husain:* O Creator and Maker of this world, I adjure Thee, by the time when the enemy threw me down from my horse, by the time when Zainab besought Shimr for mercy, though he did not allow her to close my eyes, nor permitted her to weep for me, forgive Thou graciously the evil conduct of those people, and be pleased to pardon their iniquity."

Gabriel announces the Lord's decision: He who has seen most trials, endured most afflictions, and has been most patient in his sufferings, he shall win the privilege of intercession.

He addresses the Prophet: Take this key of intercession from me, and give it to him who has undergone the greatest trials.

Of the prophets, only Jacob vies with Husain's grief and sufferings.

Gabriel reappears and, taking the verdict out of the Prophet's hands, delivers to him this message from the Lord: "None has suffered the pain and afflictions which Husain has undergone. None has, like him, been obedient in My service. As he has taken no steps save in sincerity in all that he has done, thou must put the key of Paradise in his hand. The privilege of making intercession is exclusively his. Husain is, by My peculiar grace, the mediator for all.

"*The Prophet*, handing over the key: Go thou and deliver from the flames every one who has in his life-time shed but a single tear for thee, every one who has in any way helped thee, every one who has performed a pilgrimage to thy shrine, or mourned for thee, and every one who has written tragic verse for thee. Bear each and all with thee to Paradise.

"*Husain:* O my friends, be ye relieved from grief, and come along with me to the mansions of the blest. Sorrow has past away, it is now time for joy and rest; trouble has gone by, it is the hour to be at ease and tranquillity.

"*The Sinners* (entering Paradise): God be praised! By Husain's grace we are made happy, and by his favor we are delivered from destruction. By Husain's loving-kindness is our path decked with roses and flowers. We were thorns and thistles, but are now made cedars owing to his merciful intercession." [11]

Bibliographical Notes and References

CHAPTER ONE

These books will best orient the English-speaking reader to the background, doctrine and history of Islam:

H. A. R. Gibb, *Mohammedanism. An Historical Survey.* Oxford University Press, Geoffrey Cumberlege, London, New York, Toronto, 1949. (Home University Library, vol. 197.)

P. K. Hitti, *History of the Arabs.* London: Macmillan Co., 4th ed., 1949.

H. Lammens, *Islam: Beliefs and Institutions.* London: Methuen & Co., 1929.

G. E. Von Grunebaum, *Medieval Islam. A Study in Cultural Orientation.* Chicago: Chicago University Press. 2nd printing, 1947.

T. Andrae, *Mohammed. The Man and His Faith.* London: George Allen and Unwin Ltd., 1936, is a competent and readable biography of the Prophet.

The articles in the *Encyclopaedia of Islam,* Leiden: E. J. Brill, 1913-1938 (4 vols. + Supplement) are for the most part the result of independent research and therefore of great value.

The Koran has been quoted mostly in the translation by R. Bell, *The Qur'ân.* Edinburgh: T. & T. Clark, 1937-39.

1. Gibb, *op. cit.,* pp. 62-63.
2. E. E. Calverley, *Worship in Islam.* (A translation of Ghazzâlî, *Ihyâ' 'ulûm ad-dîn,* Bk. IV.) Madras, etc.: The Christian Literature Society of India, 1925, p. 47.

3. Hujwîrî, *Kashf al-Mahjûb* (the oldest Persian treatise on Sûfism), translated by R. A. Nicholson. Leiden: E. J. Brill; London: Luzac & Co., 1911, p. 300.
4. Calverley, *op. cit.*, p. 118.
5. Hujwîrî, pp. 302-303; 303.

CHAPTER TWO

The most extensive studies on the Pilgrimage are by C. Snouck Hurgronje, *Het Mekkaansche Feest*, Leiden, E. J. Brill, 1880, and by M. Gaudefroy-Demombynes, *Le Pèlerinage à la Mekke. Étude d'histoire religieuse*, Paris, Geuthner, 1923. The Dutch scholar A. J. Wensinck has done a great deal for the interpretation of the meaning of the individual rites and for the understanding of their connections with cognate ceremonies in other Semitic religions. His studies, "The Ideas of the Western Semites Concerning the Navel of the Earth" and "Semitic Rites of Mourning and Religion. Studies on their Origin and Mutual Relations," that appeared in the *Verhandelingen der Koninklijke Akademie van Wetenschapen te Amsterdam*, Afdeeling Letterkunde, N.R., XVII/1 (1916) and XVIII/1 (1918), as well as his contributions to the *Encyclopaedia of Islam* (especially the articles *Hadjdj, Ka'ba,* and *Masdjid al-Haram*) are of the highest value. So are various papers by H. Lammens on Mecca, including his article on this city in the *Encyclopaedia*. Wensinck's monographs significantly add to, and in some instances correct, the presentation by W. Robertson Smith, *Lectures on the Religion of the Semites*, 3rd ed., by S. A. Cook, London; A. & C. Black, 1927 (who does not have much to say on the Pilgrimage); and the important chapter on the *hajj* in J. Wellhausen, *Reste arabischen Heidentums*, 2nd ed., Berlin, G. Reimer, 1897.

A selection of outstanding travelers' reports on Mecca that are easily available in English and contain more or less complete accounts of the Pilgrimage includes:

J. L. Burckhardt, *Travels in Arabia*. London, 1829. 2 vols.

Sir R. F. Burton, *Personal Narrative of a Pilgrimage to al-Madineh and Meccah*. Memorial Edition, London: Tylston & Edwards, 1893. 2 vols. (Numerous editions.)

A. J. B. Wavell, *A Modern Pilgrim in Mecca and a Siege in Sanaa*. London: Constable & Co., 1913.

E. Rutter, *The Holy Cities of Arabia*. London, New York: G. P. Putnam's Sons, 1928. 2 vols.

Lady Evelyn Cobbold, *Pilgrimage to Mecca*. London: John Murray, 1934, is interesting because of its recent date.

Two books (in Arabic) by Egyptian Muslims are of unusual importance:

Muhammad Labîb al-Batanûnî, *ar-Rihla 'l-Hijâziyya* (The Journey to Hijâz). 2nd ed., Cairo: 1329/1911.

Ibrâhîm Rif'at Pasha, *Mir'ât al-haramain* (Mirror of the Two Holy Cities). Cairo: 1344/1925. 2 vols. The author was three times *amîr al-hajj*.

E. W. Lane's masterpiece, *An Account of the Manners and Customs of the Modern Egyptians*. London, New York and Melbourne: Ward, Lock & Co., 1890 (many other editions), is inestimable for its accurate descriptions of festivals. A classic of the same rank is C. Snouck Hurgronje, *Mekka* (in German), Haag: M. Nijhoff, 1888-89. 2 vols., the second of which was translated into English by J. H. Monahan as *Mekka in the Later Part of the 19th Century*, Leiden: E. J. Brill, and London; Luzac & Co., 1931.

F. Duguet, *Le pèlerinage de la Mecque au point de vue religieux, social et sanitaire*. Paris: Rieder, 1932, has examined the Pilgrimage from the medical point of view.

1. Azraqî (d. 834 or 837) quoted by Wensinck, *Navel*, p. 18. The following quotations refer to pp. 23, 28, 51 and 21 of the same paper.
2. EI (*Encyclopaedia of Islam*), III, 438.
3. By Lammens, *ibid*.
4. Cf. Batanûnî, *op. cit.*, p. 48.
5. Burckhardt, *op. cit.*, I, 188.
6. Batanûnî, *op cit.*, p. 96; ef. also *EI*, III, 390.
7. *Oriente Moderno* (Rome), XII (1932), 458, 506.
8. Wensinck, *EI*, II, 591.
9. This description has been primarily suggested by Wensinck and Rutter.
10. Wavell, *op. cit.*, p. 130.
11. *Travels*, ed. and trans. C. Defrémery and B. R. Sanguinetti, Paris, 1853-58 (4 vols.), I, 305; Batanûnî, *op. cit.*, pp. 121-22.

12. Wensinck, *Rites*, pp. 56-57, esp. pp. 58 and 73.
13. Burton's rendering, *op. cit.*, II, 139-40.
14. Imru'ulqais (ed. W. Ahlwardt, London, 1870), 48.58b. (Imru'ulqais lived *ca.* 500-540.)
15. Rutter, *op. cit.*, I, 110.
16. *Ibid.*, I, 158.
17. Wensinck, *EI*, II, 198.
18. *Oriente Moderno*, X (1930), 84.
19. Rutter, *op. cit.*, I, 184.
20. Cf. Lady Cobbold, *op. cit.*, pp. 237-38.
21. Lane, *op. cit.*, pp. 405, 406.
22. Cf. I. Goldziher, *Revue de l'histoire des religions*, II (1880), 302.
23. *Husn al-muhâdara*, Cairo, 1299, II, 219.
24. Batanûnî, *op. cit.*, pp. 26 and 24; trans. Wensinck, *EI*, II, 588.
25. Ibn Jubair, *The Travels*, ed. W. Wright (2nd ed., revised by M. J. de Goeje); Leiden & London, 1907, pp. 132-35.
26. Batanûnî, *op. cit.*, p. 158; cf. Gaudefroy-Demombynes, *op. cit.*, pp. 222-24.
27. *Ihyâ' 'ulûm ad-dîn* (Revival of the Religious Sciences), Bûlâq, 1289/1872, I, 252-58 (Book VII, ch. 3, sect. 2; abridged). For the modern outlook cf., e.g., Muhammad Rashîd Ridà (1865-1935), in *al-Manâr* (The Lighthouse), XVI (1331/1913), 677-88.
28. Hujwîrî, *op. cit.*, p. 326.
29. *Ibid.*, p. 327.
30. L. Massignon, *Al-Hallaj. Martyr mystique de l'Islam.* Paris: Geuthner, 1922, pp. 275-76.
31. Hujwîrî, *op. cit.*, p. 327.

CHAPTER THREE

Access to juridical and other technical information with regard to the Ramadân fast will be most readily obtained through the *EI* articles on *Ramadân* (M. Plessner), *Sha'bân* (A. J. Wensinck) and *Sawm* (C. C. Berg). In his study, "Arabic New Year and the Feast of Tabernacles," in *Verhandelingen* . . . , Afd. Letterkunde, N.R., XXV/2 (1925),

Wensinck has greatly contributed to our understanding of
the Ramadân from the point of view of comparative religion.

1. Wensinck, *El*, IV, 239.
2. M. Plessner, *Handwörterbuch des Islam*, eds. A. J. Wensinck and J. H. Kramers, Leiden: E. J. Brill, 1941, p. 611.
3. Lane, *op cit.*, pp. 435, 436.
4. A. Mez, *The Renaissance of Islam*, London: Luzac & Co., 1937, p. 426.
5. Bêrûnî, *The Chronology of Ancient Nations*, trans. C. Edward Sachau, London: W. H. Allen & Co., 1879, p. 203.
6. Goldziher, *loc. cit.*, p. 308.
7. Mez, *op. cit.*, p. 425.
8. *Ihyâ'*, I, 221; the following quotations are all from Book VI, I, 221-228.
9. *El*, IV, 194 (speaking of the Shâfi'ite law-school).
10. Hujwîrî, *op. cit.*, p. 325.
11. Rutter, *op. cit.*, II, 117-20 (abridged).
12. C. Snouck Hurgronje, *Mekka*, pp. 65, 66.
13. Burton, *op. cit.*, I, 74-5.
14. *Arabia of the Wahhabis*, London: Constable & Co., 1928, pp. 11-12.
15. Lane, *op. cit.*, pp. 464; 462-63; 464.
16. E. Sell, *The Faith of Islam*, 2nd ed., London: K. Paul, Trench, Trübner & Co., 1896, pp. 319-20.

CHAPTER FOUR

There is no comprehensive study of sainthood in Islam nor
have the rich materials on Sûfism been systematically presented. T. Andrae, *Die Person Muhammeds in Lehre und
Glauben seiner Gemeinde*, Stockholm, 1918, and I. Goldziher,
"Die Heiligenverehrung in Islam," in: *Muhammedanische
Studien*, Halle/S, M. Niemeyer, 1888-90, II, 275-378, have
done the basic work with regard to the development of the
ideas concerning prophethood and sainthood. For a special
area, the important contribution by T. Canaan, *Mohammedan
Saints and Sanctuaries in Palestine*, London, Luzac & Co.,
1927, must be noted. The work of R. A. Nicholson, especially *The Mystics of Islam*, London, G. Bell & Sons, Ltd.,

1914, his lectures on *The Idea of Personality in Sufism*, Cambridge, Cambridge University Press, 1923, and *Studies in Islamic Mysticism*, Cambridge, Cambridge University Press, 1921, is probably the best introduction to Islamic mysticism.

The *Encyclopaedia of Islam* offers important articles on the subject, in particular *Walî* (Carra de Vaux), *Mawlid* (H. Fuchs), *Tasawwuf* and *Tarîka* (both by L. Massignon).

1. Nicholson, *Studies*, pp. 86, 87, 88.
2. Hujwîrî, pp. 212-13.
3. Nasafî (d. 1142) *'Aqîda*, trans. E. E. Elder, *A Commentary on the Creed of Islam* . . . , New York: Columbia University Press, 1950, pp. 138-39.
4. Cf. *EI*, IV, 1109 (Carra d Vaux), and Munâwî, *al-Kawâkib ad-durriyya*, vol. I, Cairo, 1357/1938, pp. 11-13, where twenty different types of miracles are enumerated.
5. Nicholson, *Studies*, pp. 67 and 55. The same story is told of an earlier saint, Sahl at-Tustarî (d. 896).
6. Carra de Vaux, *EI*, IV, 1110.
7. *Travels*, pp. 114-15.
8. Ibn Khallikân, *Biographical Dictionary*, trans. by McGuckin de Slane, Paris, 1843-71, II, 539-40.
9. Ibn Taimiyya, *Kitâb majmû'a fatâwî*, Cairo, 1326-29/1908-11, I, 312.
10. Cf. his *Husn al-maqsid fi 'amal al-maulid*, mss. Escorial 1545^2, ff. 29^v - 34^r, and Berlin 9544, ff. 4^v - 11^v.
11. Snouck Hurgronje, *Mecca*, p. 147; Fuchs, *EI*, III, 421.
12. Rutter, *op. cit.*, II, 196-97 (abridged).
13. F. W. Hasluck, *Christianity and Islam under the Sultans*, Oxford: Clarendon Press, 1929, I, 113.
14. Canaan, *op. cit.*, p. 284.
15. *Journal of Hellenic Studies*, XXI (1901), 203-4; cf. Hasluck, *op. cit.*, I, 274-75.
16. For the festival, cf. Canaan, *op. cit.*, pp. 193-214, esp. 199-200, 212 (where the poem is quoted); for Ibn al-Hâjj, cf. I. Goldziher, *Zeitschrift des Deutschen Palaestina-Vereins*, XVII (1894), 119-20.

CHAPTER FIVE

Perhaps the most convenient introduction to the atmosphere of the Shî'a is provided by D. M. Donaldson, *The Shî'ite Religion*, London, Luzac & Co., 1933; a competent introduction to its thought-world by R. Strothmann's article *Shî'a* in the *EI*. This is to be supplemented by the article *Ta'ziya* by the same writer. Passion plays are most easily available to the English reader in Sir L. Pelly, *The Miracle Play of Hasan and Husain*, London, 1879, 2 vols.; French renderings in A. Chodzko, *Théatre persan*, Paris, 1878.

1. *'Aqā'id ash-Shî'a* by 'Alî Asghar b. 'Alî Akbar (first half of 19th century); quoted by E. G. Browne, *A Literary History of Persia*. Vol. IV. Modern Times, Cambridge: Cambridge University Press, 1930, pp. 395 and 394.
2. Browne, *op. cit.*, p. 175.
3. Strothmann, *EI*, IV, 712.
4. B. D. Eerdmans, *Zeitschrift für Assyriologie*, IX (1894), 283-86, who describes the ceremonies as seen by J. Morier in Teheran in 1816.
5. Browne, *op. cit.*, p. 180.
6. For the details, cf. Eerdmans, *loc. cit.*, pp. 289-302.
7. W. R. Smith, *op. cit.*, p. 412.
8. Cf. Lane, *op. cit.*, pp. 392-99.
9. Strothmann, *EI*, IV, 711.
10. *EI*, IV, 712, from Chodzko, *op. cit.*, pp. 5-6.
11. The texts are selected from Pelly, *op. cit.*, II, 100-101; 335-48.

Index

'Abdalkarîm al-Jîlî, 70
'Abdalqadir al-Kîlânî, 70
Abraham, 8, 18, 19, 24, 31, 33, 47, 83
Abû Bakr, 17.
Abû Sa'îd b. abî 'l-Khair, 71
Abyssinians, 4
Adam, 19, 20
Adam and Eve, 30
adhân, 9, 61
Adonis (-Tammuz), 88, 89
Akbar, see 'Alî Akbar
'alamain, 32
'Alî, 17, 69, 73, 85, 86, 88, 91
'Alî Akbar, 91, 92
al-'îd al-kabîr, see Great Festival
al-'îd as-saghîr, see Little Festival
Allâh, 7, 9, 11, 15, 17, 20, 31, 33, 43, 44, 57, 67, 68, 70, 77, 78
Allâhu akbar, 10
amîr al-hajj, 37
Ammonites, 82
'Aqaba, 33, 47
'aqîqa, 83, 84
Arabia, 4, 36, 52
Arabian paganism, 4
Arabs, 6, 7, 27, 35, 38, 40, 53
'Arafa (or 'Arafât), 15, 31, 32, 35, 38, 40, 43, 46-48
Arbela, 73
Arch of the Banî Shaiba, 29

arkân, see Pillars of the Faith
Armenia, 89
Artemis, 38
'Ashûrâ, 51, 89
Asia Minor, 78
'asr, 60, 74, 75
auliyâ', see walî
autâd, 71
Averroes, 5

Bâb as-Safâ, 30
Bâb as-Salâm, 29
Bâb Banî Shaiba, 24
Baghdâd, 54, 70, 74
Bakka, see Mecca
Banû Shaiba, 22
baraka, 23, 38
Batanûnî, 25, 43
Bâyazîd Bistâmî, 49
Bedouin, 12, 36, 42, 43, 63
berî'a, 53
Bêrûnî, 54
bid'a (hasana), 76
bi'r, 20
Black Stone, 19, 23, 29, 46
Book, see Koran
Bubastis, 38
Burckhardt, John Lewis, 22
Burton, Sir Richard, 59, 62
büyük bairam, see Great Festival

Cairo, 37, 39, 55, 59, 65, 80, 89
Canaan, 24

Carnival, 55
Chinese shadows, 74
Christ, 92
Christianity, 4, 5, 78
Christians, 4, 5, 6, 8, 9, 20, 68, 90
Circumcision, 83
Constantinople, 37
Copts, 55

Damascus, 86
Day of Atonement, 51, 52
Day of Moistening, *see yaum at-tarwiya*
Delta, 38
Dervish, 77, 80
Devils, *see jamarât*
dhikr, 77, 82, 89
Dhu 'l-Hijja, 31, 33, 34, 35, 58
Diaspora, 4
Djidda, *see* Jidda
du'â', 10
Duldul, 88

Egypt, 22, 39, 53-55, 76, 78, 83
Egyptian government, 24
Emigration, *see hijra*
ephod, 27
Ethiopian, 21
Europe, 39
Evans, Sir Arthur, 79

Fasting, 4, 6, 51-65
Father of the Cats, 38
Fâtiha, 8, 10, 65
Fâtima, 73, 88
Fâtimids, 89
fatwà, 76, 77
finjân, 60
First Rabî', 74, 76
First Rabî', Twelfth of, 73
Friday Service, 11, 34, 58, 77

Gabriel, 6, 19, 24, 90-94
ghauth, 71
Ghazzâlî, 12, 44, 47, 56-59

Great Devil, *see* 'Aqaba
Great Festival, 34, 59, 63, 65
Great Mosque, 22, 25, 29, 30, 34, 60

Hagar, 19, 24, 31
hajj, see Pilgrimage
hâjj, 26, 28, 30, 37, 41
hâjja, 44
hajjat al-wadâ', 18
Hallâj, 48
haram, 25, 26, 30, 32, 60, 61, 78
Harâm, 22, 25
Hârûn ar-Rashîd, 73
harwal, 30, 31, 33
Hasan, 89, 91
Hasanain, Mosque of the, 89
hatîm, 24
Haurân, 83
Hebrews, 35
Hebron, 83
Herodotus, 38
Hijâz, 21, 38
hijr, 24
hijra, 7, 8, 15
Hujwîrî, 47
hulla, 27
Hurgronje, C. Snouck, 59
Husain, 86-94

Ibn al-'Arabî, 48
Ibn al-Athîr, 89
Ibn al-Hâjj, 76, 83
Ibn Battûta, 25
Ibn Fadl Allâh, 39
Ibn Jubair, 43, 73
Ibn Khallikân, 73, 76
Ibn Saud, 22, 23, 40, 41
Ibn Taimiyya, 76, 77
Ibrâhîm, *see* Abraham
'id al-adhà, see Great Festival
'id al-fitr, see Little Festival
'id al-qurbân, see Great Festival
idtibâ', 29
ifâda, 32, 33, 34

ihrâm, 26, 27, 28, 34, 36, 45, 48
ijâza, 32
imâm, 10, 61, 69, 85
imsâk, 59
India, 53, 85, 87
Indonesia, 53
Iran, 85
Iraq, 54, 85, 86, 89
Isaac, 33
Isâf, 30
'ishâ', 61
Ishmael, 18, 24, 31, 33
Islam, *passim*
Islam, Basic beliefs of, 5-6
Israel, 82
Israel, Children of, 83
Israelites, 3, 35
izâr, 26

Jabal ar-Rahma, 31
Jacob, 94
jamarât, 33, 34, 44
Jamrat al-'Aqaba, 33
Jericho, 81
Jerusalem, 8, 18, 20, 81, 83
Jesus, 3, 6, 68
Jews, 4, 5, 6, 8, 20, 79, 90
Jidda, 21, 22, 26, 39, 40
Jinn, King of the, 89, 91
Jiyâd, 59, 60
Jordan, 83
Judaism, 4, 5

Ka'ba, 18-25, 29-31, 35, 37, 42, 43, 45, 48, 60
karâma, 71, 72
Kausar, 92
Kerbela, 86-88, 90, 92, 93
Khadîja, 6
Khaizurân, 73
khatîb, 63, 64
Khuldah, 79
khutba, 11, 32, 33, 63, 73, 90
Khuzistan, 89
kiswa, 24, 37, 39
Koran, 7-11, 20, 40, 48, 52, 54, 57, 58, 60-65, 67, 68, 70

küçük bairam, see Little Festival
Kûfa, 86

labbaika, 28
lâ ilâha illâ Allâh, 5
lailat al-barâ'a, 53
lailat al-qadr, 52, 55, 57
Lane, E. W., 37, 59, 65
Last Supper, 3
Lebanon, 19
Little Festival, 59, 63-65
Little Pilgrimage, *see 'umra*
Lotus-Tree at the Boundary, 24, 53

mahmal (*mahmil*), 37, 38
majdhûb, 72
Makoraba, *see* Mecca
manâqib, 76
manhar, 35
Maqâm Ibrâhîm, 19, 24, 30, 47
maqâm's, 24
Maqdisî, 21
Mâriya, 88
Marwa, 39, 31, 46
Mas'à, 30
masjid, see Mosque
Masjid al-harâm, see Great Mosque
matâf, 24, 29
maulid (*môlid*), 73, 76, 77, 80
maulid an-nabî, 73
mauqif, 35
mausim, 81, 82
Mecca, 4-6, 8, 10, 15-22, 25, 26, 29-34, 36-53, 47, 48, 59, 73, 76, 80, 83
Meccans, 7, 77
Medina, 7, 8, 18, 20, 51, 72, 73
Mediterranean, 5, 21
me'îl, 27
Mesopotamia, 21, 73, 74, 89
mikrâb, 21
Minà (Munà), 15, 31-35, 39, 48, 59, 63

mîqât, 26
mîzâb ar-rahma, 24
Moses, 6, 35, 68
Mosque, 9, 10, 62
Mosul, 73, 74, 89
Mother of the Cats, 38
Mother of Towns, *see* Mecca
Mount Hermon, 19
Mount Hirâ, 6
Mount of Mercy, *see* Jabal ar-
 Rahma
Mount of Olives, 19, 78
Mount Thabîr, 31, 33
mu'adhdhin, 9, 61
muezzin, *see mu'adhdhin*
muftirât, 56
Muhammad, son of 'Abdal-
 lâh, of Mecca, the Prophet
 (*ca.* 571-632), *passim*
Muhammad b. al-Fadl, of
 Balkh, 48
Muhammadan era, 8, 53
Muharram, 58, 87
Muharram, First of, 53, 87
Muharram, Tenth of, 51, 52,
 85-89
muhrim, 27, 28, 33
Muhtasham, 86
multazam, 23, 30
muqarrab, 70
mushaf, 37
Mustafa, 88
mu'tamir, 28, 30
Mutawakkil, 54, 86
mutawwif, 39, 40
Muzaffar ad-Din Kökbürü,
 73-75
Muzdalifa, 32, 35, 48

nabî, 79
Nâ'ila, 30
Nasîbîn, 74
naurûz, 55
Nebî Mûsà (Moses), 81-83
New Year, 52-55
Night of Power, *see lailat
 al-qadr*

niyya, 28, 56
Noah, 93
North Africa, 83

Old Testament, 27, 28, 90
Ottoman Turks, 78

Palestine, 78, 83
Passion Play, *see ta'ziya*
Passover, 36
Pelagia, 78
Perfect Man, 70
Persia, 54, 87, 89
Persian Iraq, 74
Persians, 4
Philby, H. St. J. B., 62
Pilgrimage, 4, 6, 14-49, 53, 73
Pillars of the Faith, 5, 51
Prayer, 5, 6, 9-13, 25-28, 42,
 44, 46, 61
Prophet, *see* Muhammad, son
 of 'Abdallâh
Ptolemy, 21

Qâ'ânî, 88
qâdî, 32, 33, 56
qibla, 8, 12, 42
Quadragesima, 52
qubba, 19
Qur'ân, *see* Koran
qutb, 71
Quzah, 35

Râbi'a 'l-'Adawiyya, 78
Rajab, 36, 58
rajm, 33
rak'a, 10, 30, 61
Ramadân, 4, 6, 36, 51-65
ramal, 29
Red Sea, 21
Renan, 78
ridâ', 26, 29
Riyâd, 62
Rome, 18
Rutter, Eldon, 22, 59

Sabbath, 11
Sacrificial Feast, *see* Great
 Festival

Safâ, 30, 31, 46
Safar, 74
sahûr, 59, 60, 61
Saints, 67-84
Saladin, 73
salâm, 43
salât, see Prayer
Satan, 31, 47, 57, 71
Saturnalia, 55
Saudi Arabia, 40
saum, see Fasting
sa'y, 30, 31, 33, 36, 44
Sayyida Zainab, 80
seker bairam, see Little Festival
Selim II, Turkish Sultan, 25
Seljuq, 78
Semitic, 25, 27
Serbia, Southern, 79
Sha'bân, 56, 58
Sha'bân, Fifteenth of, 52, 53
shâdharwân, 23, 29
shahâda, 5, 10, 24, 43
Shaikh of the Camel, 38
Shaikh Mahmud, 80
Shammar, *see* Shimr
Sharîfs, 22
Shawwâl, First of, 62
Shî'a, Shî'ism, Shî'ite, 69, 73, 85-90
Shimr, 88, 90, 91, 93
Sinai, 35
Sinjâr, 74
Sitta Nefîsa, 80
Solomon, 55
Solomon, Throne of, 24
South Arabia, 21
Stoning of the Devils, *see* rajm
Sûfî, 73, 74, 75, 77
Sûfism, 69, 76
Sunnî, Sunnism, Sunnite, 73, 85, 89, 90
Sûq al-Lail, 73
sûra, 8

Suyûtî, 39, 76
Syria, 22, 54, 78

Tabernacle, 24
Tabernacles, Feast of, 29
tâbût, 89
takbîr, 27, 28
takbîrat al-ihrâm, 27
talbiya, 28, 32, 33, 45
Tan'îm, 34, 40
tarâwîh, 61, 62
tashrîq, 34, 59
tawâf, 29-31, 34, 39, 43, 44, 46, 48
ta'ziya, 89-94
Tekke, 79
Tekke Keui, 79
Tishri, Tenth of, 51
Torah, 5
Tuwaiq, 62

'Umar, 23
Umayyad, 86, 91
Umm 'Unqûd, 89
'umra, 26, 28, 29, 31, 34, 36, 43
'umrat al-wadâ', 34
Üsküb, 79

Verse of the Throne, 9

Wahhâbî, 40, 62, 77
walî, 70-72
waqf, 82
wudû', 10
wuqûf, 31-33, 35

yaum an-nahr, 33
yaum at-tarwiya, 35
Yazîd, 90, 91
Yemen, 4, 85
Yemenites, 43
Yôm Kippur, 53

Zainab, 93
Zamzam, 21, 22, 24, 30, 34, 35
zamzamî, 24
Zoroastrian, 10